Improving Disab‐
Stu‐
UNIV‐

How do disabled students feel about their time at university? What
practices and policies work and what challenges do they encounter?
How do they view staff and those providing learning support?

This book sets out to show how disabled students experience university life today. The current generation of students is the first to move
through university after the enactment of the Disability Discrimination
Act, which placed responsibility on universities to create an inclusive
environment for disabled students. The research on which the book is
based focuses on a selected group of students with a variety of impairments, as they progress through their degree courses. On the way they
encounter different styles of teaching and approaches to learning and
assessment. The diversity of their views is reflected in the issues they
raise: negotiating identities, dealing with transitions, encountering
divergent and sometimes confusing teaching and assessment.

Improving Disabled Students' Learning studies how university staff
members experience these new demands and work to widen participation and create more inclusive learning climates. It explores their
perspectives on their roles in a changing university sector. Offering
insights into the workings of universities, as seen by their central participants, its findings will be of great interest to all practitioners who
teach and support disabled students, as well as campaigners for an end
to discrimination. Crucially, it foregrounds the views of disabled students themselves, giving rise to a complex, contradictory and always
fascinating picture of university life from students whose voices are
not always heard.

**Mary Fuller, Jan Georgeson, Mick Healey, Alan Hurst, Katie Kelly,
Sheila Riddell, Hazel Roberts and Elisabet Weedon.**

Improving Learning TLRP

Series Editor: Andrew Pollard, Director of the ESRC Teaching and Learning Programme

Improving Classroom Learning with ICT
Rosamund Sutherland, Susan Robertson and Peter John

Improving Learning in College: Rethinking literacies across the curriculum (forthcoming)
Roz Ivanic, Richard Edwards, David Barton, Marilyn Martin-Jones, Zoe Fowler, Buddug Hughes, Greg Mannion, Kate Miller, Candice Satchwell and June Smith

Improving Learning in Later Life (forthcoming)
Alexandra Withnall

Improving Mathematics at Work: The need for techno-mathematical literacies (forthcoming)
Celia Hoyles, Richard Noss, Phillip Kent and Arthur Bakker

Improving Research through User Engagement (forthcoming)
Mark Rickinson, Anne Edwards and Judy Sebba

Improving the Context for Inclusion: How teachers and educational psychologists can use action research to work together to develop inclusion (forthcoming)
Sue Davies, Andrew Howes, Sam Fox, Sian Swann and Heddwen Davies

Improving What is Learned at University: An exploration of the social and organisational diversity of university education (forthcoming)
John Brennan

Improving Disabled Students' Learning (forthcoming)
Mary Fuller, Jan Georgeson, Mick Healey, Alan Hurst, Katie Kelly, Sheila Riddell, Hazel Roberts and Elisabet Weedon

Improving Working as Learning (forthcoming)
Alan Felstead, Alison Fuller, Nick Jewson and Lorna Unwin

Improving Learning by Widening Participation in Higher Education (forthcoming)
Edited by Miriam David

Improving Disabled Students' Learning

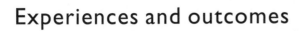

Experiences and outcomes

Mary Fuller, Jan Georgeson,
Mick Healey, Alan Hurst,
Katie Kelly, Sheila Riddell,
Hazel Roberts and
Elisabet Weedon

Routledge
Taylor & Francis Group

LONDON AND NEW YORK

First published 2009
by Routledge
2 Park Square, Milton Park, Abingdon, Oxon OX14 4RN

Simultaneously published in the USA and Canada
by Routledge
270 Madison Ave, New York, NY 10016

Routledge is an imprint of the Taylor & Francis Group, an informa business

Typeset in Charter ITC and Stone Sans by
RefineCatch Limited, Bungay, Suffolk
Printed and bound in Great Britain by
TJ International Ltd, Padstow, Cornwall

British Library Cataloguing in Publication Data
A catalogue record for this book is available from the British Library

Library of Congress Cataloging in Publication Data
p. cm.
Includes bibliographical references.
1. People with disabilities—Education (Higher)—Great Britain.
2. College students with disabilities—Great Britain.
I. Fuller, Mary, Professor.
LC4814.G7I57 2009
371.9'0474—dc22
2008052294

ISBN10: 0–415–48048–5 (hbk)
ISBN10: 0–415–48049–3 (pbk)

ISBN13: 978–0–415–48048–2 (hbk)
ISBN13: 978–0–415–48049–9 (pbk)

25306464

Contents

Illustrations

Figure

Tables

Contributors

Mary Fuller is Professor of Education at the University of Gloucestershire and Director of the ESRC/TLRP project 'Enhancing the quality and outcomes of disabled students' learning in higher education'. Her research interests are gender, race and disability in educational settings, areas in which she has published extensively.

Jan Georgeson is Senior Lecturer in Early Years Professional Status at the University of Chichester. She has worked on a variety of research projects investigating disability and disadvantage, with particular interests in organisational structure, interactional style and sociocultural approaches to pedagogy.

Mick Healey is Director of the Centre for Active Learning, University of Gloucestershire. He is internationally known for his research into teaching and learning in higher education. He is a National Teaching Fellow and a Senior Fellow of the Higher Education Academy.

Alan Hurst is formerly Professor of Education, University of Central Lancashire. Trustee of Skill: National Bureau for Students with Disabilities. He has published books and articles, and lectured and led workshops on disability in higher education in many countries. Worked with government agencies to develop and monitor policy and provision for disabled students.

Katie Kelly got her first degree from the University of Gloucestershire and went on to work in a disability rights organisation. She was Research Assistant to the project on which this book is based, focusing on data gathering for the student case studies. She has returned to working in the voluntary sector.

Sheila Riddell is Director, Centre for Research in Education Inclusion and Diversity at University of Edinburgh. Her research interests include equality and social inclusion, with particular reference to

gender, social class and disability in education, training, employment and social care. She has published extensively in these areas
and sits on policy advisory committees on disability and equal
rights.

Hazel Roberts has a research studentship at the University of
Gloucestershire. Her doctoral thesis investigates the role of support
workers in the learning process of disabled students in higher
education. She has worked as a researcher on the project on which
this book is based.

Elisabet Weedon is Deputy Director, Centre for Research in Education Inclusion and Diversity, at the University of Edinburgh. Her
main research interests are in the area of adult learning. She is
currently researching lifelong learning in Europe and learning in
the workplace, and has published research in this area.

Series editor's preface

The Improving Learning series showcases findings from projects within Economic and Social Research Council's Teaching and Learning Research Programme (TLRP), the UK's largest ever coordinated educational research initiative.

Books in the Improving Learning series are explicitly designed to support 'evidence-informed' decisions in educational practice and policymaking. In particular, they combine rigorous social and educational science with high awareness of the significance of the issues being researched.

Working closely with practitioners, organisations and agencies covering all educational sectors, the programme has supported many of the UK's best researchers to work on the direct improvement of policy and practice to support learning. Over 70 projects have been supported, covering many issues across the life course. This book is one of the first from the more recent suite of projects concerned with post-compulsory and higher education. We are proud to present the results of this work through books in the Improving Learning series.

Each book provides a concise, accessible and definitive overview of innovative findings from a TLRP investment. If more advanced information is required, the books may be used as a gateway to academic journals, monographs, websites, etc. On the other hand, shorter summaries and research briefings on key findings are also available via the programme's website at http://www.tlrp.org

We hope that you will find the analysis and findings presented in this book helpful to you in your work on improving outcomes for learners whether in government, in college or university concerned with policies, pedagogies or institutional practices.

Miriam E. David, AcSS, FRSA,
Professor and Associate Director (Higher Education),
ESRC Teaching and Learning Research Programme

Acknowledgements

This book is based on a project in the Economic and Social Research Council's (ESRC) Teaching and Learning Research Programme (TLRP) (research grant RES-139-25-0135 'Enhancing the quality and outcomes of disabled students' learning in higher education'). We are indebted to ESRC for the funding and to our colleagues in TLRP for their unfailing interest and support. In particular we would like to thank Katherine Ecclestone and Miriam David, our TLRP 'critical friends', whose active interest benefited both the research and the researchers. We would like to thank all those students who made this research possible by taking part over a period of three years. Their contributions have challenged and deepened our understanding of the lived experience of disability and what it means to be a disabled student in the UK. This book is dedicated to them. We are indebted to the lecturers who generously allowed us to observe their teaching and took time out of their busy schedules to answer our questions; also to those senior managers and disability support staff whose reflections on their universities' policies and practices underpin much of this study. We are also indebted to the following people who helped to ensure the project's successful completion: Gill Oddy, the lynchpin of the project, who contributed so much more than her role of project administrator might suggest; Andrew Bradley for his work on the surveys and who helped get the project off to a good start; Moira Peelo, whose knowledge of the issues was vital at a critical point in the project's development; and Phil Gravestock, not least for his supervision of Hazel Roberts, the PhD student attached to the project, and for good humoured advice and help at a number of key points.

Part I

What is the issue with disabled students' learning?

Chapter 1

Introduction

Mary Fuller, Sheila Riddell and Elisabet Weedon

Context

In this chapter we set out the concerns that guided the research on which the following chapters are based and the issues which the study investigated. We provide a context in terms of legislation about disability equality; summarise the main themes emerging from research studies about disabled students in higher education at the point when the study began and as it progressed; and give information about the research methodology and methods used to gather material for the following chapters.

First and foremost the book foregrounds the views of disabled students about their experiences as undergraduates, including their experience of teaching, learning and assessment as well as other aspects of student life. It solicits their opinions about what enabled or hindered their full inclusion in university life, the issues that occupied them most as they picked their way through the support they considered appropriate for their needs from what was offered to them. The book endeavours to identify the ways – big and small – in which their daily lives differ from those of their non-disabled peers. Their voices are heard in most chapters, but are the specific focus of chapters 3, 4, 6, 7 and 8.

We asked university staff to discuss their understanding of inclusive higher education, including their take on existing and developing legislative requirements in relation to disabled students. Teaching staff were asked to comment on their understanding of and position towards making reasonable adjustments in teaching and assessment, while senior managers and others with specific roles in the support of disabled students were asked to reflect on institutional policies aimed at the full inclusion of disabled students. Staff perceptions are the basis of chapters 2, 5 and 9 in particular and are incorporated into chapter 4 as well.

Starting points

The social model of disability as developed by Oliver (1990) and Barnes (1991) has been immensely important in shifting the focus of disability research from cataloguing individual deficits to developing a better understanding of the social, political and cultural barriers which exclude and marginalise disabled people. The operation of barriers for students with impairments in higher education has not been extensively explored. We assumed that barriers would involve far more than physical access, that they might operate through the construction of knowledge in a particular discipline, the working practices and common sense assumptions about knowledge, pedagogy and assessment of academics in particular departments and/or the culture of particular institutions. We were guided by the idea that the social model of disability needs to be enriched by a better understanding of the psycho-social effects of impairment (see Thomas, 1998).

The study therefore investigated the relationship between the learning environments provided in particular subject areas with the quality of learning of disabled students in each institution. Research on subject disciplines (Healey and Jenkins, 2003; Hounsell and Anderson, 2008) suggests variable practice along subject discipline lines. In building up from a detailed examination of student experience and the practice of university staff in supporting the learning of disabled students, we built on the Tavistock Institute (Cullen *et al.*, 2002: 47) review of current pedagogic research which recommended 'further studies that build upwards from practice, and encouragement for more reflexive practice and sharing of practice'.

While it is clearly of great interest to know whether there are more disabled students at university than before, this project focuses rather on whether and in what ways, having obtained a place to study at university, disabled students are fully included in higher education or are marginalised and excluded. This directs our attention to institutional and students' perceptions of barriers and facilitators, and to notions of 'fairness' rather than access. The study is concerned with the inclusion in higher education of disabled undergraduate students, who have been identified as a marginalised group (Baron *et al.*, 1996) and focuses upon their perceptions and experiences of teaching, learning and assessment. Marginalisation may take a variety of forms.

For example, within the UK, despite having qualifications comparable to those of other students when entering the same university, disabled students tend to encounter more barriers to learning and achieve poorer outcomes in terms of final degree classifications (Riddell *et al.*, 2002). The research focuses upon disabled students at a critical point in their lives as both learners and future workers, the outcomes of which will have a life-long impact for good or ill on their earning capacity and their position in the labour market.

The project involved a four-year study of disabled students (from January 2004 to December 2007) in four universities within the UK (two that achieved university status pre-1992, before the provisions of the Further and Higher Education Act 1992 came into force, and two post-1992) chosen for their different histories, prestige, size, geographical location and subject mix. Disabled students were interviewed and some of their classes observed over three years of their undergraduate careers to provide first-hand evidence of the students' experiences as undergraduates studying a variety of subjects. Evidence was also gathered from student surveys and staff interviews (see later for further details of our research methods). The research documents each university's variable achievements in creating environments that are inclusive, thus providing an institutional context in which to understand disabled students' experiences and perceptions of their time at university.

The policy context

Since September 2002 the Special Education Needs and Disability Act (SENDA) 2001, now Part 4 of the Disability Discrimination Act (hereafter, Part 4 DDA), made it unlawful to discriminate against disabled students and prospective students in all aspects of educational provision. This shifts the focus from recruitment and physical access towards the removal of barriers in relation to teaching, learning and assessment so that disability issues 'cannot remain closed within a student services arena but must become part of the mainstream learning and teaching debate' (Adams and Brown, 2000: 8). Much work in the area of disability in higher education focuses exclusively on support services (true also of the USA, see Getzel, 2008) and, while producing useful recommendations on meeting the needs of disabled students, it has had less to say about teaching, learning and assessment, or how to engage academics in incorporating the necessary processes of change in their own practice as lecturers (Hurst, 1998).

Although some statistical work has focused on examining disabled students' learning experience and attainments (Richardson, 2001) there has been little study of the specific institutional and disciplinary/departmental context in which their experience and educational outcomes occur.

Support for disabled students has expanded and is now commonly managed through centralised support units. In line with disability equality legislation, lecturers are expected to make reasonable and anticipatory adjustments to curriculum, pedagogy and assessment practices and students are legally entitled to these adjustments. The inclusion of disabled students in higher education has been supported by a number of measures, including the Disabled Students' Allowance (DSA) and premium funding intended to improve institutional accessibility. Funding Council initiatives aimed at promoting adjustments to the curriculum and to assessment, as well as quality assurance requirements, have also promoted inclusion. Part 4 DDA is important, since it placed a duty on institutions to make reasonable and anticipatory adjustments for disabled students in relation to teaching, learning and assessment. While the legislation was generally welcomed, some uncertainties remained with regard to what counts as a reasonable adjustment and who is covered by the legislation. The manifestation and impact of these uncertainties can be seen throughout the research in this book.

Apart from disability legislation there have been other major changes within UK higher education, as it has changed from being an elite system into a mass system catering for a diverse student population. These other changes are discussed in relation to universities' variable response to anti-discrimination legislation in chapter 2, which also investigates the extent to which universities in our study saw widening access to teaching, learning and assessment for disabled students as an essential part of their quality assurance agenda. Over the past two decades, higher education has transformed from an elite to a mass system, with a significant reduction in per capita funding. At the same time, new public management has grown in influence, reflected in regimes of accountability such as the Research Assessment Exercise and Teaching Quality Assessment. For example, the Quality Assurance Agency's *Code of Practice for Students with Disabilities* (1999) – whose current re-drafting is informed by the present research – was based on the assumption that ensuring access to the curriculum and pedagogy for disabled students was an essential aspect of quality assurance. The Code specified over 20 precepts with which all institutions were expected to comply, but was not intended to challenge academic freedom or to be 'prescriptive or exhaustive' and institutions might 'adapt it to their own needs, traditions, cultures and decision-making processes' (QAA, 1999: 4). Subsequently, other equalities legislation was passed, opening up university processes to closer scrutiny. Universities are required to return information to the Higher Education Statistics Agency (HESA) on the number of disabled students in specific categories and, for the purposes of establishing the level of premium funding paid to an institution, the number of DSA recipients. Part 4 DDA requires institutions to avoid discriminatory practices, and the Disability Equality Duty, which came into effect in December 2006 (and hence towards the end of this project) requires institutions to publish disability equality schemes which chart progress over time and encourages them to develop positive attitudes towards disabled people and disability issues.

Part 4 DDA is particularly radical as government has traditionally been reticent to intervene in teaching, learning and assessment practices in higher education, this being seen as a key aspect of institutional autonomy (Fender, 1996; Riddell, 1998). The onus is placed on the responsible body to know which students are disabled, while respecting confidentiality. Subsequently, universities have to define what 'reasonable adjustments' must be made to teaching, learning and assessment policies and practices and what counts as 'less favourable treatment'.

However, universities are not obliged to take steps which would compromise academic standards or be detrimental to the safety or well-being of other students or staff members. Serious questions arise about which students are entitled to reasonable adjustments and where boundaries are to be drawn in defining what constitutes a reasonable adjustment or less favourable treatment in particular areas. This may be especially difficult when defining the essential learning outcomes of particular courses and how knowledge and skills may be demonstrated through non-traditional forms of assessment (see chapter 4). It can be especially difficult in certain subject areas where professional bodies are involved in accreditation. There is evidence that disabled students are particularly under-represented in vocational areas such as education, medicine and professions allied to medicine (see chapter 7 which looks at students in our study who were involved in initial teacher training). On the other hand, some subjects which are less reliant on traditional transmission pedagogy may attract a relatively high proportion of disabled students (see Neumann *et al.*, 2002).

Our research project investigated institutional responses to the legislation, as well as highlighting areas where further guidance was required. Traditionally, students have tended not to challenge curriculum, pedagogy and assessment methods in higher education. However, the implementation of Part 4 DDA provides new opportunities for them to demand more flexible forms of teaching, learning and assessment and this research investigated the extent to which students are willing and able to adopt the role of critical consumers of curriculum and pedagogy. Our findings on this form the basis of chapters 3, 4 and 6.

Despite these external pressures to adapt teaching, learning and assessment to meet the needs of disabled students, there is virtually no literature on the types of change which have been generated. A Scottish Higher Education Funding Council-funded project led by the University of Strathclyde (SHEFC, 2000) aimed to help academic staff reflect on various aspects of delivery of the curriculum, and to change practices in order to meet the teaching and learning needs of students with a range of impairments. A project funded by the Higher Education Funding Council for England to map teaching resources for disabled students (HEFCE, 2002) concluded that very little teaching material was available then.

The policy changes mentioned earlier can be characterised as a movement away from assimilation in which practices are based on the medical model of disability whereby disabled students are provided individual support in a reactive way in order to participate in largely unchanged university courses. More recent legislation – the DDA as amended in 2001 and 2005 and the Disability Equality Duty (2006) – is in part informed by the social model of disability which emphasises that disability has to be understood in terms of barriers to inclusion rather than as individual deficit. That model, and the legislation informed by it, implies transformation of institutional practices and policies in recognition of the diversity of the student body (see Ainscow 2002) as a means of creating an inclusive institution. In brief the legislation now requires universities to make 'reasonable anticipatory adjustments' to their provision rather than making reactive accommodations which require students to declare an impairment before adjustments are made to teaching and assessment practices, as was formerly the case.

Growth in participation of disabled students in higher education: who has benefited?

Before the 1990s, universities made very little provision for disabled students. In the intervening years, many policy legislation and funding measures have been introduced, including government targets to increase the proportion of the population attending university, widening participation initiatives that are aimed at a variety of under-represented social groups and the extension of disability discrimination legislation to education, as already discussed.

These measures have led to more disabled students participating in higher education. Gorard and Smith (2006) argue that available data-sets for analysis of patterns of participation in higher education are too incomplete or flawed to establish with any confidence whether any particular group is under-represented. However, even with their flaws, they are the only sources of data that can give approximate information about the number of disabled students and the (changing) nature of their declared impairments. Table 1.1 shows that an overall increase in student numbers between 1994–95 and 2004–05 has been accompanied by a rise in the number of disabled students. Given that there is no obligation for students to report an impairment, the actual number may be higher than this table shows, perhaps closer to 10 per cent.

Composition of the group has also changed, with a considerable rise in the numbers of students with dyslexia now entering higher

Table 1.1 A comparison of known disabled students in higher education and all students (first degree programmes)

Year	No. of students (full-time in brackets)	No. of disabled students (full-time in brackets)	% disabled students (full-time in brackets)
1994–95	323,011 (273,586)	11,162 (9,719)	3.4 (3.6)
2004–05	379,150 (320,865)	26,085 (22,890)	6.9 (7.1)

Source: HESA, 2008 (www.hesa.ac.uk)

Note: The Disability Discrimination Act (DDA) defines a disabled person as someone who has a physical or mental impairment that has a substantial and long-term adverse effect on his or her ability to carry out normal day-to-day activities. There are additional provisions relating to people with progressive conditions. The DDA 2005 amended the definition of disability. It ensured that people with HIV, cancer and multiple sclerosis are covered by the DDA effectively from the point of diagnosis, rather than from the point when the condition has some adverse effect on their ability to carry out normal day-to-day activities.

education. In 1994–95 15 per cent of first degree disabled students were known to be dyslexic; in 2004–05 the proportion had risen to 50.5 per cent (if only full-time students are included this figure rises to 54.2 per cent); over the same period of time those in the category 'unseen disability' decreased considerably (see Table 1.2). These changes may be attributed to three main factors: earlier identification in the school population, support through the DSA and an increase in the number of mature students through widening access policies (National Working Party on Dyslexia in Higher Education, 1999). It seems that the overall growth in disabled students since 1994–95 has been almost exclusively as a result of including dyslexic students in the category 'disabled' (Gorard 2008; Riddell and Weedon 2006).

Research objectives and relationship to earlier studies

Building on our prior research (Fuller and Gravestock, 2002; Hurst, 1996; 1998; 1999; Riddell *et al.*, 2005) this study investigated the

Table 1.2 Categories of disability used by HESA and percentages of all disabled undergraduate students 1994–95 and 2004–05 (first degree programmes)

Type of impairment	1994–95 % of all disabled students (full-time in brackets)	2004–05 % of all disabled students (full-time in brackets)
Unseen disability	52.6 (57.5)	16.7 (17.1)
Dyslexia	15.0 (16.2)	50.5 (54.2)
Other disability	9.5 (8.9)	10.5 (10.2)
Deaf/hard of hearing	6.3 (5.9)	3.9 (3.7)
Wheelchair/mobility difficulties	5.8 (2.9)	2.8 (2.6)
Blind/partially sighted	4.0 (3.9)	2.4 (2.4)
Multiple disabilities	4.7 (3.3)	7.6 (4.8)
Mental health difficulties	1.9 (1.2)	4.6 (4.0)
Personal care support	0.2 (0.2)	0.1 (0.1)
Autistic spectrum disorder	N/a	0.8 (0.9)

Source: HESA, 2008 (www.hesa.ac.uk)

nature of the barriers encountered by students with specific disabilities in particular institutions and disciplines. It also investigated teaching staff's changing practices in particular institutions, their success in removing barriers and the impact of these changes on the performance and educational experience of disabled students.

The project aimed to obtain students' first-hand experiences of reasonable adjustments and lecturers' perspectives on making such adjustments to their teaching and assessment practices. Consequently this study incorporates important evidence gained from disabled students themselves about understanding how policies and practices hinder or facilitate student learning, and from students and lecturers about how legislative requirements may challenge existing pedagogical practices.

Reviewing literature before we began the study (Borland and James, 1999; Freewood and Spriggs, 2003; Hall and Tinklin, 1998; Holloway, 2001; Hurst 1998; Riddell, 1998; Tinklin and Hall, 1999) we noted a number of gaps:

- There were no longitudinal qualitative studies of how students with different impairments experience study programmes in higher education;
- Students with particular impairments (e.g. hidden disabilities and mental health problems) were absent from many studies;
- There had been virtually no analysis of the academic performance of disabled students compared with non-disabled peers;
- Studies were commonly a-theoretical, failing to problematise assumptions about teaching, learning and assessment;
- We lacked understanding of how institutional policies and practices in teaching, learning and assessment have responded to the challenges posed by disability equality legislation and the demands of politicised disabled students.

Our longitudinal in-depth project addressed some of these gaps by using Schutz's (1932) concepts of taken-for-granted knowledge to explore disabled students' and lecturers' implicit understandings of existing teaching, learning and assessment practices, and their responses to legal requirements for changes in them. We sought the opinions and experiences of a wide range of undergraduates, including those with unseen disabilities including mental health problems. In addition to producing in-depth data with regard to students' and lecturers' understandings of teaching, learning and assessment practices in particular institutions, we looked across four institutions to gain insights into the way in which specific environments produce particular understandings of and approaches to teaching, learning and assessment. We also sought to understand the ways in which implicit knowledge may be challenged by attempts to introduce innovative practices in teaching, learning and assessment.

There was no existing work which develops theory in relation to teaching, learning and assessment practices as applied to disabled students. This project drew on a variety of theoretical frameworks (Baumard, 1999; Berger and Luckman, 1972; Schutz, 1932 [1972]; Trowler and Cooper, 2002) in its early stages. In attempting to provide some understandings of how approaches to teaching, learning and assessment are socially determined in particular subject, disciplinary and organisational contexts we have found Activity Theory (Engeström, 1987) a fruitful basis for analysis (see chapter 9).

Taking into account this earlier body of work, the main aim of this study was to understand how disabled students' academic perform-ance and experience of teaching, learning and assessment vary by disability, subject studied and type of institution, how this experience develops during their course and how their learning outcomes com-pare with those of non-disabled students. A survey of all self-disclosed disabled students in four selected universities at the beginning of the project gave rise to an analysis of similarities and differences in their experiences of barriers and opportunities in teaching, learning and assessment. Institutional case studies and case studies of individual disabled students afforded an opportunity to examine the relationship between the quality of learning of disabled students and the learning environments provided by specific departments in the selected uni-versities as well as to analyse the extent to which disabled students' learning outcomes differ from those of non-disabled students. Inter-views with teaching staff and observation of some teaching sessions enabled us to document and analyse their understandings of teaching, learning and assessment and changes made to their teaching, learning and assessment strategies in the light of the legal requirement to make 'reasonable adjustments'.

Research methods

The research investigated the following overarching questions:

- How do disabled students in specific institutions experience teaching, learning and assessment practices in particular subject areas?
- How do changes in teaching, learning and assessment affect their performance and outcomes over time?

As a means of addressing the questions the study also asked:

- What are the learning and educational outcomes of disabled students, as measured by retention rates and academic achievements, in comparison with non-disabled students?
- How do teaching and other staff understand and interpret disability equality legislation in relation to teaching, learning and assessment?
- To what extent do staff interpretations accord with or challenge existing implicit knowledge about teaching, learning and assessment?
- What impact did recent policy and legislative developments aimed at the inclusion of disabled students appear to have on teaching, learning and assessment policy and practice in particular institutions over time?
- How can the quality and outcomes of learning of disabled students be enhanced?

We gathered material in the following ways:

- A survey of attitudes and barriers to learning of all disabled students in the four universities, with a matched sample of non-disabled students for comparison in one university;
- Document analysis and key informant interviews in the four universities to investigate differences in policy and practice with regard to disabled students' learning and assessment, leading to institutional case studies;
- Interviews at various points in time over three years with 31 disabled students, leading to longitudinal individual case studies of their learning experiences during the course of their undergraduate studies;

- Interviews with academic staff who taught one or more of the disabled students in the longitudinal study and observations of learning environments;
- Analysis of the degree outcomes of disabled students in comparison with the wider student body, using each university's data.

We investigated whether the pattern of performance of disabled and non-disabled students in pre- and post-1992 universities was similar or different, whether students with particular impairments performed better or worse than either students with different impairments or than non-disabled students. Students' performance may depend on variables other than impairment: we asked about how they defined their social class, and noted students' gender, ethnicity and age. This material is summarised in Appendix A.1 but the diversity of the students means that we do not systematically report on social class, age, gender and ethnicity when discussing their performance. Aggregated data were obtained from three universities on the degree outcomes of graduating disabled students compared with those of other graduates. Only outcome data was available for participating students at University 4.

Institutional case studies

Statistics relating to a range of demographic variables and institutional documents on widening access and provision for disabled students were gathered and analysed from each university. In order to interpret these data, a total of 28 key informant interviews were carried out: ten in University 1, six in University 2, seven in University 3 and five in University 4. Of these, ten were senior managers, either deans, heads of school or staff responsible for teaching and learning; nine were senior staff managing libraries, IT systems, university estates and student accommodation; two were involved with student services but with an additional remit for disabled students; and six were involved with services for disabled students. Some of this material has already been published (Riddell *et al.*, 2007).

Table 1.3 summarises the characteristics of the four participating universities. There are significant differences in the proportion of students from less socially advantaged backgrounds, University 1 having by far the most socially advantaged intake. There are also differences in the proportion of students disclosing a disability (see Table 1.4),

Table 1.3 Key characteristics of the four universities

University	Type of institution	No. of undergraduate entrants		Student population				
		Total	Young (18–25)	% from schools	% low participation neighbourhood	% from social class III, IV and V	% in receipt of DSA	% disclosed disability 2003–04
1	Scottish, Pre-1992	3,785	3,340 88.3%	65.7	8.9	17.8	2.8	6.0
2	English, Pre-1992	2,355	1,365 73.2%	90.7	10.2	19.0	2.1	5.3
3	English, Post-1992	1,835	1,365 74.3%	94.2	12.5	31.1	3.2	10.0
4	English, Post-1992	4,920	3,140 63.8%	96.6	19.2	36.2	3.2	4.3 (2002–03)

Source: Institutions' own data

Table 1.4 Number of students who disclosed an impairment to Universities 1, 2, 3 and 4 by type of impairment and percentage of all disabled students: UCAS categories (2003–04)

Impairment/learning disability	University 1		University 2		University 3		University 4	
Dyslexia	657	52%	196*	46%	351	49%	467	42%
Wheelchair/mobility impaired	28	2%	16	4%	22	3%	71	6%
Unseen impairment	271	21%	62	14%	195	27%	120	11%
Other impairment (specified)	168	13%	0	0%	65	9%	224	20%
Blind/partially sighted	29	2%	21	5%	17	2%	33	3%
Personal care	0	0%	5	1%	1	0.1%	3	0.3%
Multiple impairments	28	2%	23	5%	15	2%	81	7%
Deaf/hard of hearing	53	4%	16	4%	30	4%	81	7%
Mental health difficulty	35	3%	7	2%	18	3%	28	3%
A disability not listed/no details/not known	0	0%	83	19%	5	1%	0	0%
Total disabled	1269	6%	429	5.3%	719	10%	1,108	4.3**

Source: Institutions' own data 2003–04

Notes: * Students classified as having learning difficulties and dyslexia
** Calculated as a percentage of the number of all undergraduate students including part-time students

Table 1.5 Institutional support for disabled students

Institution	Type of support
University 1	Disability Office, with 6 members of staff, 1 administrator, includes 2 dyslexia specialists
University 2	Includes Disability Service and a specialist language and learning support unit
University 3	Disability Office, 2 full-time advisers, part-time administrator
University 4	Disability Office, 5 part-time advisors, 1 with responsibility for deaf/hard-of-hearing students and 1 for students with mental health difficulties

Source: Institutions' key informants and documentation 2003–04

with University 3 having the most. In all four universities, students with a diagnosis of dyslexia represent by far the largest group.

Each university provides specialised disability support (Table 1.5).

Survey of students

In spring 2004 we conducted a survey of all disabled undergraduate students in the four selected universities. The questionnaire was developed to capture disabled students' experiences of barriers and inclusive practice (Fuller, Hurst and Bradley, 2004). A total of 2,572 questionnaires were sent out with 1,171 returned. The overall survey return rate was 45 per cent, with some variation between the different institutions. Forty per cent of the respondents were male, 60 per cent were female and 70 per cent of the sample were aged 25 or below. In order to compare the experiences of disabled and non-disabled students, the questionnaire was administered to a 10 per cent sample of non-disabled students (n=272). A 40 per cent response rate was achieved. Responses of 602 dyslexic students specifically were analysed separately and reported in Weedon and Riddell (2007a), as they represented by far the largest group and were identified by lecturers as posing particular challenges in terms of adjustments to pedagogical and assessment practices.

Individual student case studies

We initially hoped to track 48 disabled students throughout the course of their studies. However, difficulties arose in contacting disabled students in some institutions as a result of confidentiality issues, and there was also some attrition of students who initially agreed to participate in the study but then dropped out (sometimes leaving university altogether) as a result of work and social pressures. Researchers at each institution were responsible for collating material from student interviews, staff interviews and teaching observations into individual case studies for each student. Three years' data were obtained for 31 students (see Appendix A.1 for student details). The breakdown of the student as per university attended is as follows:

* University 1 (pre-1992): 14
* University 2 (pre-1992):   4
* University 3 (post-1992): 8
* University 4 (post-1992): 5

Once the four institutional and 31 individual student case studies had been drawn up they became a resource for all project researchers. In the following chapters researchers draw on material from all four universities and all case study students except in chapter 2 which analyses the experience of disability at the institutional level, chapter 7 which focuses on extended vignettes of two students in one university and chapter 9 where a single institutional case study provides the material for an analysis of dilemmas and contradictions in policy and practice for the support of disabled students.

A note on names, disciplines and universities

As is already obvious from this chapter, each university is referred to by a number. All student and staff names have been anonymised and staff roles presented in a simplified way as either lecturer, senior manager or disability support officer. Staff informants who are quoted in the following chapters are listed, along with their institution and disciplinary affiliation in Appendix A.2. Where giving the exact title of a discipline or course risks compromising anonymity we have used a more generic label. For Universities 2, 3 and 4 we have used the convention of giving staff and students names beginning with the same letter, as follows: University 2 names beginning with C, University 3 names beginning with D, University 4 names beginning with B. Staff at University 1 have names beginning with A, but students are variously named (though not with names beginning with B, C or D).

Part II

What our research study tells us

Chapter 2

Managerialism and equalities

Tensions within widening access policy and practice for disabled students in UK universities

Sheila Riddell and Elisabet Weedon

New Labour's public policy agenda, in education as elsewhere, has been driven by the twin goals of widening access and raising attainment through the implementation of new managerialist policies and practices. New public management has its origins in a neo-liberal philosophy which holds that all human behaviour can and should be measured and – in order to achieve efficiency, effectiveness and value for money in the public sector – all activity should be measured against agreed targets (Deakin, 1994; Clarke and Newman, 1997). The higher education sector exemplifies this approach, where targets have been set by Higher Education Funding Council for England (HEFCE) in relation to, for example, student retention and completion rates which feature in league tables.

In addition there has been an ongoing concern with widening access, and UK universities have new duties to comply with equality policies. Sex, race and disability legislation places duties on them to avoid discrimination in these areas, and HEFCE publishes benchmarks relating to 'under-represented' groups of students, with the expectation that institutions will take steps to 'converge' on their benchmarks.

In this chapter, we consider the ways in which widening access policies for disabled students, informed by both managerialist and social justice principles, are playing out in four very different university contexts.

Disabled students in higher education

There have been major changes in the nature and mode of operation of British higher education institutions over the past two decades. Student numbers more than doubled between the mid-1980s and the mid-1990s, while the unit of resource fell by a third. The middle classes benefited disproportionately from this expansion (Archer, 2003) and continued to dominate the old universities and, to a lesser extent, the post-1992 universities. Reay (2003) noted that, even in the most accessible institutions, the majority of students are middle class (for example, working-class students make up 41 per cent of undergraduates at the University of Bolton). Despite this middle-class dominance, the university student body is now more heterogeneous, with a growth in the number of mature and part-time students as well as those from minority ethnic and working-class backgrounds. Disabled students have also benefited from the expansion, making up about 5 per cent of home students, still well below the proportion of disabled people in the population (Riddell and Banks, 2001). Although patterns of participation in relation to social class, gender, ethnicity and geographical location have been widely discussed (Paterson, 1997; Osborne, 1999; Archer, 2003; Hayton and Paczuska, 2002), the participation rate of disabled students has often been omitted from analysis.

As noted in chapter 1, before 1993 higher education was largely inaccessible to disabled people and any adjustments made were at the goodwill of staff and students (Barnes, 1991; Leicester and Lovell, 1994). Since 1993 the Scottish and English Higher Education Funding Councils (SHEFC and HEFCE) were persuaded by pressure groups such as Skill: National Bureau for Students with Disabilities to offer special initiative funding to institutions to improve their provision for disabled students.

The Funding Councils have now moved towards mainstreaming funding for disabled students. Premium funding was introduced in 1999–2000 in England and 2000–01 in Scotland and is currently paid to institutions on the basis of students claiming Disabled Student Allowance (DSA). DSA is paid to individual students to cover the cost of equipment and non-medical personal help necessary to enable equity in access to education. This new way of allocating funds is mirrored in the premium funding allocated to institutions on the basis of the number of students recruited from low participation neighbourhoods. It acknowledges that there is a cost to the institution of recruiting and retaining 'non-traditional' students.

On the one hand, these measures could be seen as pathologising 'non-traditional' students; however, institutions attracting relatively large numbers of 'access' students maintain that this activity should be financially incentivised, just as research is incentivised by the Research Assessment Exercise (RAE). It could also be argued that the DSA reflects an individualised view of disability as residing within the student, which is somewhat at odds with social model thinking. Premium funding, on the other hand, reflects the need to remove institutional barriers and therefore could be seen as more attuned to the thinking of the disability movement.

The additional needs of disabled students were also noted in the reviews of higher education carried out by the Dearing and Garrick committees (NCIHE, 1997a; 1997b). These reports did not initially include disabled students in their terms of reference (Hurst, 1996); however, due in part to pressure from Skill, a number of disability-related recommendations emerged from these reports, including the need to fund learning support in universities, the need for the Institute for Learning and Teaching (ILT, now the Higher Education Academy) to include the learning needs of disabled students in their programmes and the extension of the DSA (Hurst, 1999). Disability is also featured separately in the Quality Assurance Agency's (QAA) Code of Practice for Students with Disabilities and HEFCE now publishes benchmark data relating to disability, indicating the percentage of disabled students in each institution and comparing participation with comparable institutions.

There are ongoing debates about whether devices associated with 'new managerialism' (Clarke and Newman, 1997), such as equality audits and target-setting, are capable of promoting social justice goals (Clarke *et al.*, 2000; Exworthy and Halford, 1999). Critics of the new management regimes that are intended to foster accountability and transparency maintain that they may simply be used to limit the creativity of professionals, distort performance by encouraging minimal compliance with targets and ultimately breed a climate of mistrust (Power, 1997). Proponents of the new management regimes argue that effective public services can only be delivered when appropriate goals and values are identified and targets used to assess progress.

The quality inspection process introduced in the 1990s was bitterly resisted by the traditional universities, but generally accepted by the post-1992 universities, which had been used to closer scrutiny and regulation by the Council for National Academic Awards. Subject benchmarking, also a product of the early 1990s, was resisted strongly in the pre-1992 universities on the grounds that the Government was trying to introduce a national curriculum into higher education. Farwell noted that 'the benchmark monster turned out to be toothless' (2002: 157), with most subjects producing a set of bland outcomes to which any degree course in the country would be able to conform. In many of these debates, the elite institutions maintained that their academic freedom was being eroded with a 'dumbing down' of higher education taking place.

In addition to management regimes, legislation has been used to make discrimination against disabled students unlawful. Part 4 of the Disability Discrimination Act (DDA), implemented in 2002, made it unlawful to discriminate against disabled students. Discrimination was defined as (i) failure to make reasonable adjustments for a disabled student or (ii) providing less favourable treatment to a disabled student for a reason relating to their disability without justification. Institutions were expected to carry out anticipatory adjustments, rather than simply make *ad hoc* adjustments as the need arose. From December 2006, higher education institutions were required to comply with the Disability Act, which places a duty on public sector institutions to actively promote equality for disabled people, demonstrating progress in relation to targets.

Here, too, there are debates about the potential of disability equality legislation to enhance the position of disabled people in the UK (Gooding, 2000; Meager and Hurstfield, 2005). The DDA was seen as being of great symbolic importance in recognising the political claims of disabled people. However, there is continued unease within the disability movement about the definition of disability within the Act, the justifications for failing to make reasonable adjustments or providing less favourable treatment, and the extent to which the legislative route is an effective way for disabled people to achieve justice. In addition, there is a growing debate about the extent to which academic standards are compromised by reasonable adjustments and whether making adjustments can be seen as being fair to all students (Sharp and Earle, 2000). One aspect of this project that provides the focus for this chapter therefore examines the impact of legislation at the institutional level through interviews with key informants.

Characteristics of the four universities

Details of the four case study universities are provided in chapter 1. To recap briefly, University 1 is a large ancient university with a high proportion of students from the independent school sector. University 2 is a medium-sized pre-1992 university with a less socially advantaged intake than University 1. University 3 is a small post-1992 institution with a relatively high proportion of students from the independent sector. University 4 is a large post-1992 university with a relatively high proportion of less advantaged students. All four institutions have well-developed support for disabled students, and Universities 1 and 3 have strong support for students with a diagnosis of dyslexia. This chapter draws on interviews with institutional-level key informants, further details of whom are provided in chapter 1. To maintain confidentiality, each respondent is only identified by their institution and their role as senior manager, senior support officer or disability support officer. In addition, each respondent has been allocated a pseudonym so that quotes can be attributed to a specific person.

Disabled students and the widening access agenda: policy drivers at institutional level

Informants were asked about how policy and practice for disabled students fitted into the widening access agenda. University 1 had been encouraged by the Funding Council to make greater efforts to meet its targets in relation to the proportion of students from state schools and socially disadvantaged backgrounds which had had a powerful effect in shaping the institutional response. An equal opportunities management information group provided an annual audit of the student profile in relation to Funding Council targets, considering social class, gender, ethnicity and age. Whereas the convenor of the disability committee felt that disability was a key part of the widening access agenda, two senior managers considered that, since disabled students were unlikely to be more disadvantaged than others, they should not be included within the general widening access agenda which focused on students from low participation neighbourhoods.

In terms of key policy drivers, the DDA was regarded as being of major importance: '. . . if something is in law then you have to do something about it' (Senior Manager Ackroyd).

> Then . . . the DDA also came into force and . . . it is not perfect, but it has been a fantastic platform to work from . . . I can say to people that the rights of disabled people are now enshrined in legislation . . . it is not a welfare issue any more.
>
> (Disability Support Officer Abbot)

However, it was evident that some senior members of staff were not entirely committed to the widening access agenda, partly because they did not believe that institutional policy should be managed by the Funding Council:

Very few people are going to get up and say so 'I don't wish to help disabled students graduate', and they don't, but when they are overworked anyway, all kinds of new initiatives are coming along from all sides you know, and the amount of change there's been in this university as you know in the past is just terrific. Some of it is self-induced but a lot of it is external, huge quality assurance requirements, doubling the number of students, not in the last year or two but only about ten years ago . . . all that kind of thing. Then to be asked to go to a lot of trouble for the sake of an individual, or something that will only come up every four or five years, that is a bit of a last straw sometimes.

(Senior Manager Arnold)

When asked whether there was tension in relation to the widening access agenda, a member of senior management observed:

There is enormous tension there yes . . . you let in a lot of students who perhaps weren't really as good and can't do the basic stuff and there is a possibility that the other students suffer because you are spending all the time teaching the first consignment how to spell or how to do simple maths in case of a scientist like myself, or something like that. And I think the real problem here is actually what priority people give it in their hearts and I suspect it's fairly low. Since we are all human, most of us are nice, priority goes up when you are actually confronted by the real live student, but when you are not I think that is low priority as it must be in virtually all institutions.

(Senior Manager Arnold)

Arnold, a senior manager at University 1 went on to state:

I am a great believer in the individual universities being left to sort out their own priorities given after all the legislation that there is in this area. I mean if there were no legislation in this area and there was evidence that universities were being dilatory, I can see it would be a reasonable role for the funding council. But since nobody, I don't think, would deny that the legislation in itself is fairly demanding, I can't see there's much role for the funding councils, . . . I think we should make those decisions.

(Senior Manager Arnold)

A rather different view was presented by another senior manager, who suggested that while there was genuine commitment within the university to widening access for disabled students, there were at least three inhibiting factors:

> Policies inhibiting inclusion – health and safety, we have got some glorious things to do with fire regulations ... RAE probably inhibits it because anything that we require which involves members of academic staff to go an extra mile for a particular student makes it harder for them to deliver on another agenda that we say they have to go an extra mile or two on. And I think a third set of policies that inhibit social inclusion ... are to do with the efficiency gain culture. You have to do more with less, more with less, more with less. Very hard in that context to say we have got to take even more of our money to upgrade our buildings.
>
> (Senior Manager Austen)

Whereas resentment at the intervention of the Funding Council in internal affairs was strongly expressed, others felt that senior managers within the institution had a real commitment to widening access for disabled students because they felt that it was 'the right thing to do', rather than simply being a Funding Council requirement.

Whereas the significance of internal policy drivers was stressed at University 1, senior staff at University 2 considered that, in addition to the DDA, the internal climate of the university was crucial in shaping developments. Informants explained that, in the past, institutional policy was shaped organically by members of the equalities committee, with gender having a particularly strong profile because of staff concerns and interests. Following a major financial crisis, the emphasis now was much more on formal compliance than enthusiastic engagement:

> I think the university has ... lived or is living on its past glories. It's not too bad but it's no longer kind of out there at the front ... I think there has been a relative stagnation in terms of the numbers of disabled students that we were able to recruit. I think it's also in terms of, you know the university again, probably, you may know some of this – it's entered into folklore – hit very difficult financial circumstances and that undoubtedly impacted in all kinds of ways on the resource available, on what was seen as being a cost-effective way of recruiting students, on the priorities that one

gives to non-traditional students and I think we're still kind of working that through.

(Senior Manager Collins)

The disability support officer said that senior management was increasingly concerned with managing risk 'of falling numbers, or money, or litigation, or reputation', while university lecturers felt under pressure and therefore might not 'take ownership' of the widening access and equalities agenda. While the DDA was important in ensuring compliance, some degree of commitment from staff was necessary for real change to embed:

> We have to take serious notice of compliance but I think we would be an impoverished institution if all we ever did was say, 'Okay, our aims and goals are whatever's on the compliance agenda at the moment.'

(Senior Manager Clark)

Informants at University 3, a post-1992 institution, had very different views of the quality assurance and widening access agendas compared with those at the two pre-1992 universities. Disabled students were seen to lie at the heart of efforts to widen access to university:

> As far as I am concerned in terms of actually looking at the curriculum and in terms of social class issues, there has been very little done in the country, let alone here. If anything, our focus has been on trying to support disabled students and accessibility here.

(Senior Manager Dobson)

One senior manager spoke of the efforts made by the university to be recognised as a good place for students with particular impairments, such as dyslexia:

> I think a lot of students come to us because they know we are fairly sympathetic about dyslexia ... So I think people know, and I think it is out and about in the community. Strangely enough, it cuts across bits of the access and widening participation agenda. Friends of mine who have got children who may be at minor public schools or independent schools, also think that we're pretty sensitive and sympathetic to students who've got dyslexia, and they put students in our particular way. So I think

there are different bits of the market which have a view about how we support students . . . and I think they might come for different sorts of disabilities from different places, because of that reputation.

(Senior Manager Dent)

In addition, quality assurance was not characterised as a resented intrusion, but as a relatively benign regime promoting the interests of disabled students:

I think that the QAA's Code of Practice is interesting. I think of it as the carrot, whereas the legislation was the stick version . . . Quality Enhancement [QE] is a way to really make the policies effective. I think QE is very effective amongst academic staff when activity aligns with their principles and most academic staff here would be in principle very keen to support disabled students . . . The QE has to be of such a nature that people see that it is as worthwhile in that it enables them to do their jobs more effectively, and not to be seen as one more thing that they have to do.

(Senior Manager Dobson)

The DDA, on the other hand, while a strong driving force, was regarded with some degree of fear:

I like to think that it was all based on principle. But I actually think that it is driven by anti-discrimination legislation.

(Senior Manager Dobson)

Whereas the RAE was seen as a major institutional policy driver in the pre-1992 universities, this was not the case in University 3:

I did wonder whether the emphasis on the RAE might inadvertently or overtly influence some academic staff to focus on research and not to attend to the quality enhancement aspects of their learning and teaching work. In that sense, some of them might be 'too busy' to come to the workshops on the accessible curriculum because they were focusing on research.

(Senior Manager Dobson)

For the senior manager quoted hereafter, a powerful shaping force within the institution over coming years was likely to be the growth of the personalisation agenda:

> I know this is difficult with large groups, but all students are individuals, and people have individual needs, and we have to meet these different individual needs. It's not only disabled students, other students need at different times special arrangements and I see this as all part and parcel of good teaching, and I think we haven't seen anything yet. I think with greater customisation, whatever you like to call it, we're just seeing the tip of the iceberg at the moment.
>
> (Senior Manager Dent)

As noted earlier, University 4 was the institution with the highest proportion of students from disadvantaged backgrounds, and widening access was seen as a key element of its provision:

> We genuinely believe in bringing in students who are able to study and achieve regardless of disability. We actively encourage applications from those groups . . . We have always been regarded as an institution that does attract and encourage students from areas that have students who would not normally enter higher education . . . they may be students from families who have no tradition of higher education, or they may be students who have learning disabilities, or from disadvantaged backgrounds or have disabilities and have reservations about education.
>
> (Senior Manager Bennett)

The particular part of the widening access agenda affecting the institution was the pressure from the Funding Councils to improve retention rates:

> Anyone can benefit from coming to do a degree – but are they actually going to get the degree? . . . We have a good record for widening access but even we have to make a decision that you cannot take everybody who applies.
>
> (Senior Manager Brown)

In the light of a difficult financial regime, University 4 had a major problem in deciding the proportion of its budget to be allocated to disabled students:

The law says you must not discriminate on the grounds of disability and it does say that if the cost is too great that can be grounds for discrimination but it doesn't give any clear guidance. We have tried to make a rational basis for the budget that we will make available for students with a disability and this is the basis for how we will take chunks out for the individual. But that is one area that has caused a lot of head scratching. The legal advice is utterly hopeless. For overseas students the most turgid piece of prose I have ever seen has been added into the institutional agreements saying you do your bit and we'll do ours within the law. I suspect it's meaningless.

(Senior Manager Bridge)

In the following section, we explore the impact of institutional approaches to widening access on teaching, learning and assessment policy for disabled students.

Teaching, learning and assessment policy and disabled students

A key aspect of Part 4 of the DDA is the requirement for reasonable adjustments to be made to the curriculum and assessment for disabled students in order to ensure they are not discriminated against. University 1 had participated in the Teachability project, a staff development programme intended to encourage staff to improve curriculum accessibility. While some departments had invested resources in the programme and were enthusiastic about developing it further, others had not become involved at all. A concern amongst a group of staff was whether the time and effort involved in making the curriculum accessible for a small group of disabled students was worth it, in the light of the numerous other pressures they faced:

There are real problems about the extent to which you are justifying, for example, putting on a very complicated teaching or assessment load that is very very demanding on staff for the sake of one student [referring to a case of a profoundly deaf student] ... if you look at it rationally in a way the amount of effort required to get this woman to pass through the course was actually phenomenal.

(Senior Manager Arnold)

It was noted, however, that staff in the department housing the deaf student later commented that reasonable adjustments had been made and had worked very well: 'We did it and it was great' (Senior Manager Arnold).

The willingness of staff to adapt their teaching and learning practices to meet the needs of disabled students was said to be very varied:

> You have a lot of people who have very liberal or advanced ways of thinking but then there are also these sort of dyed in the wool people 'this is the way we have always done things and always will' . . . because it is an ancient institution and it has got its traditions.
>
> (Disability Support Officer Abbot)

A number of staff spoke of the difficulties raised by certain types of impairment which might be difficult to assess reliably and might result in unfair treatment for other students:

> I think in my experience dyslexia is problematic not when people's problems are to do with spelling, that's easy to deal with that, it's clearly a problem if their problem is to do with reading. On the other hand we can cope with blind students who can't read but there are some varieties of dyslexia which seem to shade into difficulties which were not just in a sense lexical. That's really problematic . . . And I don't want to sound suspicious about classifications of dyslexia but . . . one does get a little suspicious at the margins. One of the brightest students I have ever taught in my life was classically and hopelessly dyslexic, did all his exams on a computer, I wrote him the strongest reference and the next thing he did brilliantly. I have no problems in a sense with the classical dyslexic but there are some grey areas here and the growing numbers make me a bit anxious.
>
> (Senior Manager Austen)

The strongest caveat in relation to the compatibility of maintaining standards with including more disabled students was expressed by one of the senior managers, who described the tension between the widening access agenda and the quality assurance agenda as 'irreconcilable': 'Maintaining standards in a proper way and admitting some classes of disabled students is very, very difficult to do' (Senior Manager Arnold).

At University 2, the other pre-1992 institution, there was also some degree of anxiety around assessments and standards. According to one disability support officer, staff were being encouraged to develop alternative forms of assessment, but also needed to train students in how to use these approaches effectively, otherwise disabled students might inadvertently be disadvantaged. The difference between departments was also emphasised:

> There are some departments where there are individuals who are very strong and supportive and there are some departments which are either under pressure or who have a culture that students must be very independent and get on with their own work – or where the curriculum is just difficult to adapt.
>
> (Disability Support Officer Crossley)

There was some discussion of the circumstances in which disabled students should have additional help compared to other students who were finding the course difficult. A view expressed here was that alternatives should be available to all students, not just disabled students:

> I know some people who have dyslexia and they can always use the computers for their work, well then the difficulty comes when they've got a spell checker, now how do you define where someone should be allowed to use a spell checker, where will you penalise a student who hasn't? I personally believe that everybody should be allowed to use a spell checker.
>
> (Senior Manager Dalton)

The disability advisor reported that the issue of standards and equity for disabled students had been tackled head on when the QAA Code of Practice was being compiled:

> It's something which came up quite a bit, for example, when we were writing the QAA Code of Practice on students with disabilities that I had a hand in, it was quite accepted . . . that however much you wanted to widen access, the integrity of the academic award had to have equal status, so you couldn't say, 'We feel very, very sorry for you, we'll reduce the standards and let you in.' If you didn't think that the student truly had potential to do the course, you could make adjustments to take account of things that were closely related to the impairment but you couldn't wholesale say 'We feel very, very sorry for you, we'll let you in'.
>
> (Disability Support Officer Crossley)

In University 3, one of the post-1992 universities, rather different views were presented in relation to making alternative adjustments. One respondent emphasised the need for much greater adaptation of assessment methods. The three-hour examination, he noted, might be relatively rarely be appropriate, and yet was the stock in trade of much university assessment. Professional judgment should be paramount, so that individual academics decided when it was appropriate to vary the type of assessment, with these variations being available to all students: 'I am just surprised at this question actually about what counts as reasonable adjustments because I think that you use your professional judgment about learning outcomes that have to be met' (Senior Manager Dalton).

However, another senior member of staff believed that, even though university policy was clear, there was still too much laxity on the adjustments made by individual academics:

> I do suspect that there probably is a slight possibility that these kinds of mark adjustments do go on in some of the darker corners of the university . . . I think if students make these errors after they've had the extra time, or after they've had the opportunity for someone to read through their coursework – you know, the kind of things we encourage – if those errors are still there, then I think you have to mark according to exactly the same criteria. If they're writing an essay in English, you know, and style is clearly going to be an element, then I think it's only reasonable for that to be reflected in the marks.
>
> (Senior Manager Dalton)

Further issues arose in relation to the need for customised and personalised assessment in the climate of finite and limited resources, and the particular problems which arose in professional subject areas, for example, the need to meet strict deadlines in journalism, which might be very difficult for disabled students. Finally, some trade union members wanted water-tight procedures to protect their members, a demand incompatible with the spirit of the DDA, which stated that approaches had to relate to individual students, rather than reflecting generalisations about particular categories of student.

In University 4, similar concerns were expressed about whether adjustments to assessment conferred unfair advantage on disabled students, and it was evident that again there was a wide spectrum of opinion amongst staff:

Lecturers who object to making special arrangements do make their feelings felt. Where exams are used there is a reluctance to use other forms of assessment and 25 percent extra for dyslexics is questioned by some. Other staff would use other forms of assessment. Computers were used for exams in this department for probably the first time last year.

(Disability Support Officer Burns)

Whether examinations could be dispensed with entirely for some students and whether assessments could be done at home were subjects of debate. Generally, it appeared that University 4 took a fairly conservative stance on these matters:

Our view was that it was appropriate to have an individual room and comfort items, but not appropriate to have exams at home. A similar sort of thing was about not having exams at all. Our basic approach was that if an invigilated, constrained time assessment was important to this module then in general that is what should be done. It is pretty rare for us to allow alternative assessments. Our approach is we don't want to give people an unfair advantage.

(Senior Manager Bridge)

Summary and conclusions

Respondents in the four institutions expressed rather different views with regard to the position of disabled students in relation to the widening participation agenda and the nature of the key policy drivers within the institution. In the two pre-1992 universities, disabled students were only loosely associated with the widening access agenda and University 1 had a particularly strong focus on students from socially disadvantaged backgrounds at least in part as a result of Funding Council pressure. In University 4, including students from low participation neighbourhoods was a major focus of activity because this was seen as an institutional strength. Only in University 3, a new university with a relatively advantaged social profile were disabled students seen as being at the forefront of the widening access agenda. In relation to institution-wide policy drivers affecting widening access, all respondents recognised the significance of the DDA as providing a major impulse to action.

The quality assurance regime was resented in the two pre-1992 institutions, being characterised as encouraging routine compliance or, alternatively, as an example of unwanted intrusion by the Funding Council on the university's autonomy. The RAE was seen in these universities as a major policy driver, focusing staff attention on research with the implication that they had less time and energy for supporting individual students. In University 4, the focus was on the drive to improve retention rates, which was having an impact on admissions policy, with less tolerance for students who might fail to complete the programme. Internal events also had an impact, and the financial crisis of the 1990s was clearly still in the recent collective memory of the staff at University 2, with the suggestion that managerialism was more prominent within the institution and staff less engaged with the institution's mission.

Staff were asked to discuss the nature of adjustments to teaching and assessment made as a result of the DDA, the QAA's Code of Practice and the broad approach to widening access within the institution. Relatively little was said about adjustments to the curriculum, with one institution participating in the Teachability programme, albeit with varied engagement across the university. Respondents had much more to say about assessment, and in all four institutions a considerable level of anxiety was evident. Some concerns were to do with the cost of making adjustments, but there were also major anxieties about conferring unfair advantage to disabled students in comparison with other students who were having difficulty with the course. The challenge to standards posed by students with certain impairments, particularly dyslexia, was noted, and this was a particular anxiety in the ancient university. Chapter 4 explores the perspectives on assessment of the disabled students and lecturing staff taking part in our study.

The questions posed at the start of this chapter concerned the extent to which the new managerialist agenda has been successful in achieving social justice goals in higher education, in this case, in relation to disabled students. The answer appears to be a qualified affirmative. All institutions saw the DDA as a major shaping influence, and no institution wished to be found in breach of the legislation and publicly shamed through a court case. The downside was that respondents spoke of their fears of frivolous complaints being made, and were anxious about the amount of time they might have to spend in dealing with such cases.

Pre-1992 and post-1992 institutions responded slightly differently to the demands of the quality assurance agenda. The old universities, with a greater degree of traditional autonomy, were highly resentful of what they regarded as meddling in their internal affairs, whereas the post-1992 universities, more used to central direction, were less resistant. However, there were reminders that passive compliance did not mean that major changes would ensue, and it appeared that staff enthusiasm for making major changes to the curriculum and assessment was limited, particularly in the pre-1992 institutions where the RAE was a major policy driver. In relation to assessment, change was also impeded by fears of the erosion of standards, particularly in the ancient university, and worries over privileging one group of students over another. This view was particularly apparent in University 4, where students from severely disadvantaged backgrounds were likely to experience difficulties with traditional forms of assessment, but could only claim adjustments if certified as disabled. The preference here was for making adjustments for a much wider group.

Finally, the importance of local factors appeared to be a major element in determining the effect of national policies. Respondents described the particularities of their university culture, the particular events which had shaped their recent history and the climate of specific departments. This serves as a strong reminder that changes in institutions tend to take place as a result of bottom-up, as well as top-down pressures, and the idiosyncrasies of particular institutions will make a major difference to how national policies are played out.

Chapter 3

Listening to disabled students on teaching, learning and reasonable adjustments

Hazel Roberts

The voice of disabled students is increasingly being heard, as their experiences of higher education have been a subject of interest to researchers for over a decade. However, many studies have considered the disabled student 'experience' of university without any concerted focus on what are key activities for any university: teaching and learning. Previous research into the disabled student experience of university has tended to focus on physical and attitudinal barriers to accessing higher education (Baron *et al.*, 1996; Borland and James, 1999; Tinklin and Hall, 1999), or more specialised areas, e.g. employment of personal assistants (Parker, 1999); negotiation of environments and identities (Low, 1996); and the experiences of students with learning difficulties (Boxall *et al.*, 2004).

Where teaching and learning have been considered as a significant part of the university careers of disabled students, some research has studied specific aspects such as access to support for learning in the form of reasonable adjustments (Hall and Tinklin, 1998; Riddell *et al.*, 2002) and fieldwork (Hall and Healey, 2005). However, studies are emerging that focus on the overall experience of teaching and learning for disabled students (Fuller, Bradley and Healey 2004; Fuller, Hurst and Bradley, 2004; Healey *et al.*, 2006; Jacklin *et al.*, 2007).

The project that is the subject of this book has sought to build on this work by documenting the experiences of a cohort of 31 disabled students throughout three years of their course across four institutions in England and Scotland. Interviews with these students form the main source material for this chapter, which seeks to foreground the voice of the disabled student by outlining their experiences of teaching and learning in their own words, including any adjustments made, and relationships with staff and other students.

Previous studies linked to this project have not found systematic or

significant differences between the way that non-disabled and disabled students learn within higher education (Fuller, Bradley and
Healey, 2004; Fuller *et al.*, 2004; Healey *et al.*, 2006). While some
impairment-related effects on student learning have been identified,
these can vary greatly between individual learners. Fuller, Bradley
and Healey (2004) suggest that such differences are more likely to be
caused by barriers to learning for disabled students, and emphasise
the importance of positive staff attitudes and making information
about support available. This chapter therefore focuses on areas
where significant differences have been found between the teaching
and learning experience of disabled students and their non-disabled
peers and how barriers related to these differences might be
removed.

Students' perception of their impairment in relation to learning

This section considers how students' impairments affected their
learning. Many students had clearly reflected on how they like to
learn, exhibiting diverse learning preferences that meant there was
no definitive learning style attributable to any individual impairment. However, several related their impairment(s) (or the effects of
their impairment(s)) directly to their learning, in both negative and
positive ways. Other students felt that their impairment raised
barriers to their learning rather than impacting directly on their
learning style.

It was common for students who had been diagnosed with dyslexia
to identify with the idea of a 'dyslexic learner' and relate this to their
own experience of teaching and learning. For example, Barry seemed
to have developed a very clear idea of what a 'dyslexic learner' is like
by the end of his course:

> Dyslexics are more spatially aware and more three dimensional
> than we are two dimensional, . . . they're more, rather than flat
> paper and academic orientated, they see things from an abstract
> perspective and they look at things from the outside rather than
> being on the inside.
>
> (Barry)

> My feelings about presentations are just 'no'! But . . . when
> you're not a good planner, and you have to speak fluidly, in a

very conjoined way, that doesn't always happen with a dyslexic person.

(Barry)

It was particularly common for students to raise issues around organisation in relation to dyslexia. For example, Ben felt that his difficulties with organisational skills might be due to dyslexia: 'Being dyslexic it took a while to get sorted . . . I do forget things and it is just trying to remember and then going down and doing things.'

Conversely, Barry felt that being dyslexic meant that he had to be better organised in order to cope with the demands of his course:

> I've always had to make greater provision than the normal mainstream student, way early on. I won't leave it until the last minute and get caught out . . . I research everything thoroughly then I know the brief that's going to come on . . . I've already done the spadework so I'm taking pressure off myself.

(Barry)

Barry's point illustrates that despite common assumptions that planning and organisation are difficult areas for dyslexic learners, students with dyslexia had frequently developed sophisticated organisational strategies, although it could be argued that these were necessary to address the students' inherent difficulties with organisation. For example Cara, who has dyslexia, used weekly and daily plans to help her stay organised:

> Every day I set aside a subject and worked through the notes. Memory is the worst. I have to make weekly plans now. On Sunday night I have to sit down with my diary and type up in Word even my lectures or to check mail. I started that when I got here because there is so much going on. I carry around a piece of A4 paper and cross it off when I do it.

(Cara)

Andrew talked about how his impairment (cerebral palsy) impacted on his organisation and study skills:

> I was never very good at the whole studying thing, my study skills were always bad along with my organisation . . . I was always

missing, maybe only a day or so, a deadline and then, it wasn't until I finally told my college tutor what was going on that she finally realised it wasn't me, that that was part of my disability and everything. It wasn't the fact that I was lazy or anything it was just me, always need that extra day.

(Andrew)

Ironically, disabled students are often expected (or expect themselves) to be more organised than their non-disabled peers, as Daisy noted:

You have to be double organised really and I honestly think being a disabled student actually makes your life harder and taking the support makes your life harder because you have to be more organised the whole time. There's no point me doing an assignment the night before when my support tutor needs to see it.

(Daisy)

The two students taking part in the study who disclosed diabetes both raised concentration as an issue for their learning:

Sometimes if I get too high blood sugars then it is very hard to keep my mind focused on one thing . . . It is fairly hard to keep it at a critical level.

(Alan)

Around exam time is when it gets really crazy because you need to be going into an exam, your blood sugar level needs to be perfect and if it is too low it will mess up your concentration levels in different ways . . . if you are high, . . . I think your brain overworks and goes a bit crazy but if you are low . . . you don't really see things on the paper. Things start to blur and you shake.

(Kathryn)

Some students indicated that their impairment had affected their choice of subject at university level. For example, Ben's choice of computing meant that his handwriting was less important as he could type his academic work. In response to the interview question 'so you don't consider yourself to be a disabled student?', Ben responded:

No, not really, but I think that's mostly because of the course I'm doing. Because I've managed to do something to almost get around it. So it's something that's, it's there, but it's not relevant to my work.

(Ben)

In contrast, Brandon did not feel that his dyslexia had impacted on his module choices:

I don't think it's because of my dyslexia, it's just my ability overall. My dyslexia will have an effect I guess. There are some subjects I know that some people just don't get, full stop.

(Brandon)

As well as the direct effect of impairment on learning, students also discussed other barriers to learning that their impairment presented. For example, Kathryn thought that diabetes caused problems of attendance directly affecting her learning. Similarly, Dermot considered that his main impairment-related challenge was attendance after an epileptic seizure:

I think the main thing that I find challenging would be having a fit and then getting in for a lecture . . . Maybe even having a fit and getting in for a lecture the next day, because I still feel rough the day after. So, that could be a problem for me, but apart from that, everything should be ok.

(Dermot)

Dalia, a wheelchair user, did not need any special arrangements academically but had continual problems accessing classrooms because lifts were frequently out of order. She could not access any of the teaching for a core module, and as a result had to change her major subject:

There was this problem with [module code] . . . it's upstairs in the learning centre, i.e. you can only get to it with one lift and that always breaks. And so I ended up abandoning the entire module but it was a compulsory module.

(Dalia)

When staff held mistaken beliefs about a student's learning style based on their impairment this could adversely affect student learning and cause upset. Ben related an example from school:

I did have one teacher in secondary school who insisted on giving me stuff on different coloured paper, and I was like, 'thanks, it made no difference, I can read'.

(Ben)

Brandon related a distressing experience from his first year at university:

One of the lecturers who was sitting in on my [exam] took it upon himself to read the entire maths exam test out . . . nice enough guy – but he's read this entire A plus 2 to the power of . . . and I said, 'well I can see that!' and it just really pissed me off and I said 'no, I'll ask you when I need you to read something'. And he's 'no, no, I'd better read it all out', and this is eating into my time and I was just enraged and I was nearly on the point of walking out . . . The thing is, it's lack of knowledge, they just don't know.

(Brandon)

These examples make clear the value of staff responding flexibly to individual students' learning needs, rather than adopting a 'blanket' approach based solely on their perceptions of a particular impairment.

Teaching and learning activities

Students commonly preferred a mixture of teaching and learning activities, such as a combination of lectures and seminars, rather than one single format. This preference for mixed teaching methods was also linked to a preference not to experience one single activity or teaching format over a long period of time. For Dionne this was important as she had to employ pain management techniques for her stomach condition during lectures:

You get to a stage and it's like right, count to 10 and take a deep breath, and it will be all right . . . especially when lectures go on and on, and you think actually I just want to go home . . . but I've got to sit through it.

(Dionne)

Lectures and lecture notes

Lectures are a major teaching delivery tool within higher education and all of the students had experienced lectures at some point in their course. Several singled out passive lectures as their worst-case teaching scenario, and preferred more interactive methods:

> A very long lecture where the lecturer talks at you with no slides or anything . . . because I hate taking notes and I think everyone hates taking notes. But you know, when he just talks at you . . . and you do very little in the way of supporting media, you just tend to sleep.
>
> (Dalia)

> I don't like straight lectures . . . my worst is lecturers that just talk at you because then you can't listen to them and type and think about it, you're just literally just trying to do what they're saying. Even if they're standing up there flicking their PowerPoints and making you copy it. You're not listening, you're just copying.
>
> (Daisy)

On the other hand, some of the means adopted by lecturers to provide variety in lectures could cause problems. Daisy found in-class reading exercises in lectures particularly difficult:

> That's another nightmare, no way, that's awful . . . we had that in one of our [subject] lectures, 'read this and then comment on it in class'; no, I can't do that because it takes ages to read things and I have to highlight things and then . . . no, I don't like that.
>
> (Daisy)

Lecture notes frequently emerged as a key teaching and learning issue for students and formed an important part of the lecture experience. Several students (including Dalia above) made it clear that they found taking notes to be problematic or even a barrier to their learning:

> I can't listen and notetake, I miss so much.
>
> (Barry)

> If you've got a notetaker with you then they're brilliant because you can understand and take it in, they do the writing, if you're on your own then it's a bit of a nightmare.
>
> (Daisy)

I'm not really one that can sort of hear words and take notes at the same time. So if you put it on a board I can sort of scribble down notes, but when it's a constant flowing of talk, it's sort of a no go type thing.

(Dermot)

In practice, lecture note provision could vary widely across departments, institutions and year of study. For example, in Billy's department at University 4 no lecture notes were handed out, so students had to take all notes themselves. In Kathryn's department at University 1 dyslexic and visually impaired students were routinely provided with better quality lecture information than other students, and as someone with diabetes she did not feel that this was entirely fair:

[The lecture notes] weren't as complete as the set that the dyslexia people have received [and] we would need that actual material that they got, because . . . he is kind of throwing information at you and you couldn't take that down.

(Kathryn)

Students from all four institutions found it very helpful to be given lecture notes in advance:

I can listen to the lecture and remember. We get lots of handouts and notes, which is good for me because rather than look at my notes I can look at theirs.

(Brandon)

[Lecture notes help] because you can take them to the lecture with you and then instead of having to write and listen at the same time [. . .] you have got the main teaching points anyway and you listen out for them and then you make extra notes at the side. It's a lot easier to keep up.

(Andrew)

Most lecturers put it up there ahead of the lecture. Some people on the other hand just put it up literally about 5 minutes before the lecture which doesn't give you much of a chance to sort of print them out, or look over them or whatever before the lecture which is a bit annoying.

(Darren)

I want to do something about the lecture notes not always being guaranteed to be up before the lecture. If they are not up you don't know if you have to take loads of notes or not. If they take a week to go up it's too long – you have forgotten.

(Cara)

Provision of lecture notes in advance was particularly helpful for some students who had to take time out for reasons related to their impairment:

It definitely helps. I've actually downloaded them all onto my laptop, it means that if I do miss it I can actually sit there and read through it and, unfortunately you sort of don't get what teachers have said, and they could have sort of said, well, actually, this bit isn't fully correct but you sort of still get the gist of what they are trying to say for that lecture.

(Dermot)

Dermot clearly recognised that the quality of his learning might be diminished by not attending lectures, even if he received a copy of the notes. Chapter 5 discusses concerns from staff and students that attendance at lectures would decrease if notes were routinely available in advance, and Lecturer Abercromby also questions the value of giving lectures if handouts are given out beforehand. The challenge for staff is to ensure that attending lectures gives 'added value' beyond having a copy of the lecture notes while trying to accommodate students like Dermot for whom non-attendance at lectures is sometimes unavoidable.

Fieldwork

Billy found fieldwork sessions to be the most problematic aspect of his degree, particularly in years one and two when he had problems walking long distances and with carrying equipment because he had to use a walking stick (Year 1), and crutches for a time (Year 2):

There's been projects where . . . there's a hell of a lot of walking involved, and people are carrying equipment and I've got the walking stick, and I can't carry equipment and I'm feeling different. But I guess the people working with us was ok, and they're quite understanding really. I learnt my way round it. I told my tutor, if people are walking for a long distance, I said 'I'll go on my bike'

(Billy)

While Billy developed the coping strategy of using his bike to help him with fieldwork, he did have the extra work of planning how to transport equipment and allowing himself extra time if he needed it for any offsite project. The support of his fieldwork tutor was particularly important to Billy whose experience underlines the importance of staff and peer support when students are experiencing difficulties, as well as the extra planning and organisation that can be associated with being a disabled student:

The tutor he were great because he always made sure and said, 'right we're going for a walk . . . are you okay?' It was brilliant . . . it was real beneficial for him to take that in consideration.

(Billy)

Daisy selected her field week module as an instance of not feeling well-supported. She did not have a notetaker with her and did not receive the notes she was promised either:

The lecturer did say people take notes for me, I never actually got them, got given to me either in the field or afterwards. So I don't know if that's my fault for not following it up or just . . . Well they were asked to [share their notes] but I think everybody was finding it difficult to know what to take notes on.

(Daisy)

Disabled students generally have to make difficult decisions about how and when to negotiate support. Daisy clearly found it hard to pursue the missing notes, both with her lecturer and with her student peers.

Placements

Chapter 7 explores the work placement experiences of two Initial Teacher Training (ITT) students in more detail. However, most disabled students interviewed who had the opportunity to go on a course placement chose not to do so, for reasons that varied from finance to wanting to stay with their peer group, and did not seem directly related to impairment. Dalia's experience was different as she believed that doing a year-long placement as part of her course would lead to losing her incapacity benefit:

> No. Because, if I do, I lose all my disability benefits, and ... I won't be able to get them back again ... You've got to be under 21 when you start claiming or, not in work, or, you have to have like, a sick period and then you can start claiming again ... but you're only allowed to work up to 12 hours a week, or, full time for 6 months, in a year.

> (Dalia)

For Karrie, the year abroad was an essential part of the course and she could not graduate without it, but it was not clear throughout her second year whether the placement would actually go ahead. She found sorting out all aspects of the placement to be a tortuous process – as a wheelchair user with cerebral palsy she needed suitable accommodation, a personal assistant who would stay for the year and a school that was accessible but different bodies were responsible for different parts of the arrangements:

> It ... depends on finding suitable accommodation which is proving a bit of a stumbling block. So it could all fall through if they can't find that. You know, it's not just as easy as for the other average student just to go off to Spain.

> (Karrie)

Karrie and Dalia's experiences (and those of Jean and Andrew discussed in chapter 7) show that student placements can be particularly challenging for disabled students and raise issues regarding the responsibility of universities for arranging placements and ensuring that their students are not discriminated against.

Adjustments to learning

Disabled students participating in this project accessed a range of different types of adjustments, including computers, software, printing and photocopying allowances, paper and ink cartridges for printing, book allowances, notetakers, dyslexia tutors, study skills tuition, personal helpers, dictaphones, minidisks, and extra time and use of computers in exams. Additional support with cost implications was usually paid for through the Disabled Students Allowance (DSA). Such institutional support was however contingent upon the student declaring an impairment and being assessed as requiring support by the institution or some other university approved organisation.

Students were generally positive when describing the support they did receive, and found disability service staff helpful. For example, Ben, who received extra time in exams and had stickers to put on his work to alert tutors to his dyslexia, was very happy with the amount of support he had received:

> Anything that I did ask for, just with help or if I could get anything done [such as] the stickers and things, then they just provided those. So I was well pleased.
>
> (Ben)

However, student learning support provision was often not put in place at commencement of study but relied on students being proactive about accessing it. It often seemed a matter of chance whether students were offered the support to which they were entitled. To outline just two examples, while Alan was initially offered disabled student accommodation, he was offered extra time in exams only from the end of his second year. Andrew accessed no learning support in his first year but received extra time in exams and a photocopying allowance from his second year.

Students in this study were often unsure about the support available and their entitlements, which made them less likely to be proactive about disclosing and requesting reasonable adjustments. For example, Cara received DSA for computer equipment and photocopying allowances but was unsure whether she was claiming her full allowance. She thought she might be entitled to a book allowance but was unsure exactly how to claim, so did not pursue it.

Students often did not use all the support to which they were entitled and the take up of particular types of support was related to individual needs and preferences. For example, Daisy rarely used her seven-day assignment extension but did use extra time in exams:

> Normally no I don't plan for extra time at all, unless it's an exam, and then I do. Because essays then, no, it usually gets handed in the day it says in the module guide about 90 per cent of the time. But exams are different anyway, you plan for the extra time because you need to, to get it finished, it's as simple as that.
>
> (Daisy)

Dalia did not feel that she needed an extension for her assignments:

> I was offered a seven-day extension and it was like, hang on, wheelchair does not affect my ability to hand things in on time!
>
> (Dalia)

While Dalia makes a valid point, it is clear that the extra organisational work involved with being a disabled student at university has the potential to affect their performance and ability to hand work in on time, even if ostensibly their impairment should have no impact in this respect.

Organising support

While institutions are often seen as the primary administrators of disability support, disabled students were expected to spend a significant amount of time organising their support. The irony of this for students experiencing impairment-related barriers to their learning has already been noted. Daisy described the first week of a semester as 'hell':

> Well you do have to go and see the disability advisor and say this is my timetable, I want notetakers for this and then the notetakers either email or phone you and say can you meet me there? I've obviously got a different notetaker and then, my support worker, you email her and she says, are you free here, here and here, when would suit you? So you do have to go and re-establish your contacts, make sure the disability advisors have your timetable.
>
> (Daisy)

Barry also found it time-consuming to establish support:

> In the first year there was a lot of things I needed to be put in place like my glasses with a prism in, the dark tint, the dyslexia training, the computer training for the software they give us. The first year was quite time-consuming because I had to find spaces for all this in between lectures, but when I conquered that and I did in the first year I was pretty chuffed with myself then because I'd filled in so much around my course when a normal mainstream student would just have to do the course.
>
> (Barry)

Organisational tasks often centred on the DSA. Students raised a range of specific issues around accessing and receiving learning support that were linked to the administration of DSA. Dalia and Barry both described their disillusionment with the system:

> When I need software for the course, I can't just go out and buy it, I have to say to [disability advisor], 'I need the software for this module', then she sends a letter to the LEA [Local Education Authority], then the LEA buy it, no, the LEA research where's cheapest to buy it, then they send me a letter that I have to sign and send back to them to say that the money can come out of the funds, and then eventually I get my software. And in the meantime the course has finished! It seems unnecessarily convoluted really . . . It would be so much easier for me to phone up and say 'can I buy this software', or even phone the LEA and say 'can I buy this software for my course'.
>
> (Dalia)

> There is a flaw, the fact that there's a space of time between the initial entry to your course, and getting the funding, or the disability people assessing me by the psychologist. And that gap is crucial, because that's like your introductory few months into the course, whereby you want to make that a smooth transition . . . The first two or three months is crucial, because you're talking timetables, you're talking planning, you're talking all kinds, which dyslexics aren't good at.
>
> (Barry)

In addition to lengthy delays, students also found the DSA inflexible in responding to their needs:

> They said . . . have the assessment, you don't have to agree to anything. So, I had the assessment and they said, we think you need this chair and this desk adaption [sic], this, that and the other. Ok, you can think it away because I don't! [laughs]. However, he then put the recommendation into [assessment centre], who ordered the stuff and now I'm in a big argument because I don't actually want this stuff . . . And they're like 'but you need it!' and I'm like 'no, I don't'!
>
> (Dalia)

We've also found that my disabled student's allowance was meant to get me a laptop with a far bigger hard-drive than it actually does . . . and I said 'look, I needed a laptop with a large hard-drive because of the nature of the course I'm doing' . . . and they said 'Oh well you accepted that one' and it's like, 'I accepted all three of the ones you offered me because I didn't understand the system and you wouldn't explain it'.

(Dalia)

Brandon was sceptical generally about how much he benefited from the DSA as a disabled student:

It seems ridiculous to me, that you get absolutely nothing [at school] and you get flourished with all these absolutely useless gifts [at university] a minidisk player with a microphone, which I've never used . . . I was given a computer with some software, for this that and the other, a printer, I can claim back ink cartridges, I get a photocopying and printing allowance at the university, all of which I've never used to be honest . . . I mean, I've been given ink cartridges, it doesn't make any difference, you know, if I am poor that would make a difference, but being dyslexic it doesn't make a difference.

(Brandon)

Linked to this perception of unfairness, several students made it clear that they did not want to claim more learning support than they actually needed. Kathryn thought it was unfair for her to claim DSA because others had a greater need than she did:

I don't need any extra money for anything in particular so I don't think it would be fair . . . I just don't see what I would do that would merit having an allowance. Do you know what I mean? I don't see what I could buy to aid my study further. Unless you are talking about food but this is stupid because everyone eats food! It is not the sort of thing that merits having an allowance. You'd much rather it was people who really need it.

(Kathryn)

The experience of students participating in this project demonstrates that it is clearly inappropriate to provide 'blanket' adjustments according to type of impairment, where no account is taken of students' individual learning needs and preferences. Building up a dialogue with students about their personal requirements and being flexible in the provision of support seems likely to create considerable resource-efficiency savings and ensure support is targeted more effectively.

The administration of information about student disability

Appropriate information management once students have disclosed an impairment is a central requirement under disability discrimination legislation. However, several students raised concerns relating to confidentiality when it came to accessing support. Brandon gave one example:

> There's a sheet that goes round all the appropriate departments telling them about me I guess and [it was] a bit annoying. When I was looking for something in the workshop down in the [subject] area and it was just on someone's desk in the middle for everyone to see. So I removed it and sort of asked what's it doing . . . I didn't really get a good response but it was sort of, well everyone was given them and it shouldn't have been there, sorry . . . and that was it.
>
> (Brandon)

In Cara's experience it seemed to be individual students' responsibility to let lecturers know about their disability status which she thought might be due to concerns about confidentiality:

> They don't tend to make them aware of who is and who isn't, you have to go and tell them . . . in terms of the actual staff unless you directly tell them, they don't know . . . I think they're worried about confidentiality, but yeah, you don't need the admin staff to know . . . It's the people who are dealing with marking your work or teaching you that really needs to know. But I think it's confidentiality reasons.
>
> (Cara)

One very common assumption made by students was that disclosing an impairment on the student UCAS application form meant that disability staff would be proactive in contacting them and that their teaching staff would be informed, but this was often not the case (although legally the institution would have been deemed to have been informed of the student's disability). For example, Teresa wrongly assumed that disclosure meant that her course team knew about her impairment. She had no contact with University 1's Disability Office until her second year. Before that point she had spent a lot of time seeking extensions and getting doctor's notes for individual assignments.

Relationships with staff – positive and negative experiences

> There's no ideal style. Some lecturers can carry some things off some can't, some people make you more interested and some make you want to go to sleep, some lecturers are more sensitive than others, some are more organised than others. A lot of it's down to them, it really is.
>
> (Daisy)

Chapter 2 has already noted variability in the willingness of staff to adapt their teaching and learning practices to meet the needs of disabled students. This is confirmed by the experiences of disabled students taking part in the project. As already noted, irrespective of institutional policy, in practice students often needed to inform staff individually about their impairment(s) before any reasonable adjustments were made which could lead to lengthy delays in adjustments being put in place.

Students described the majority of their relationships with staff in positive terms. The most common staff attributes they identified as important were helpfulness, availability, approachability and being supportive. Brandon spoke positively about staff at University 4 in the light of disclosing his dyslexia:

> [The academic staff have supported me] superbly. They all understand, they're all willing to flex a little bit and if you ever need help just appear at their office and they're always willing to give some help.
>
> (Brandon)

Andrew felt that he could approach some academic staff and not others:

> It depends on the lecturer. The likes of [name] in language

I would have no problem telling her anything about that because she is the type of lecturer who would understand fully. Whereas you have got the other ones and you think no, they actually think you are just stalling or looking for something for nothing . . . I don't want them to look at me differently in any way.

(Andrew)

However, students were more likely to relate individual experiences with staff where they had experienced problems, particularly when staff did not display the positive attributes identified earlier.

Particularly common issues were when students found staff to be unavailable, unhelpful or felt that course material or assignments were not explained sufficiently:

Absolutely couldn't get hold of her at all . . . and you know, people had been emailing her, saying 'is this what we're meant to do, is this right?' and most of them said never even got back to them or if they did it was very, very vague and they weren't any more clearer.

(Cara)

I emailed him and said I don't know what I'm meant to be doing for the assignment can I talk to you about it out of lecture. 'No, no my student contact time is during the lecture.' I was like, actually I think you'll find that I am paying you and eventually he saw me and basically verbally told me what was in the module guide and that helped me absolutely nothing.

(Dalia)

Cara related one example of a friend who was investigated by the institution's harassment team for emailing her tutor too much, which made Cara cautious, partly because she felt that the problem may have been due to her friend's dyslexia:

She's also dyslexic, so it's like, 'well maybe I didn't phrase it very well', so maybe he's misinterpreted . . . They dropped it and explained back to the lecturer but of course she never got on with that lecturer again and specifically chose modules that he wasn't teaching because she just felt awkward . . . it makes you feel a bit uneasy about emailing them.

(Cara)

Two ITT students at University 1 (Andrew and Jean) had an initial experience of unhelpful staff at the Disability Office before they were able to access support. Andrew felt that his negative experience might have been because he had an unseen impairment. However, his experience in the second year was a lot more positive:

> I think obviously because you don't always see my impairment you are thinking 'is there actually anything wrong with you?' And I think that's maybe where the disability advisor [in first year] and I got off on the wrong foot because she couldn't see and she thought I must be kidding here . . . I got that feeling but I never ever challenged her on it, maybe I should have done.
>
> (Andrew)

> I have spoken to a different person this year who has given me all the help in the world that I needed to get what I wanted and what I needed to help with the course. So that negative experience last year in the first instance is very positive this year. But even the lady I spoke to this time didn't understand why the other person was so negative. That does confuse me because she was a disability advisor.
>
> (Andrew)

Dalia also had a negative experience with disability support when she injured her shoulder and required extra support:

> I pulled a muscle in my shoulder and the disability advisor said 'you know, you ever need anything just let me know' I said 'well, it would be really helpful to have someone helping me get around because I just was in pain every time I pushed myself' . . . and . . . 'no-one's in the office at the moment and the disability advisor can get back to you next week' and didn't, and didn't, and didn't, and, by then it was the end of term . . . Like three weeks.
>
> (Dalia)

Students with dyslexia tutors found them particularly useful and tended to develop close working relationships. Daisy found her support worker invaluable, while Cara considered her dyslexia tutor in Years 2 and 3 very supportive in terms of both learning and personal issues:

> I couldn't do without my support worker, let's put it that way . . .

support, proof reading, drafting, I go to her. Notetakers, in some cases yes, in some cases I could have passed the module without. But if she didn't read my work then there's no way I'd pass anything.

(Daisy)

I see him every week . . . it's a lot better, at the moment it's just to help with doing essays and stuff, but he also helps me out with like personal things and, I'm getting down because I can't do something and he reassures me, so . . . that's quite good help, gives me a bit of a boost, I think.

(Cara)

Cara's tutor was her first point of contact for support, as they had regular scheduled weekly meetings and she described him as her 'disability advisor'. Her tutor was also particularly helpful when assisting her to devise strategies to cope with panic attacks in exams. Daisy and Cara's experiences demonstrate how important staff can be as a source of support to individuals. However, if the disabling barriers they encountered in their studies were not in place they would be less likely to be reliant on the generosity and time of individual staff and more likely to feel more empowered as learners.

Summary

The disabled student experience of teaching and learning at university is complex and multi-faceted. Students related many positive experiences, but understandably tended to focus on areas where problems arose. The fundamental learning differences between disabled and non-disabled students were barriers in the form of lack of provision of reasonable adjustments, and also the extra organisational work that being a disabled student implied. While dyslexic learners were particularly likely to relate their 'impairment' to their learning style, for other disabled students it was the disabling effects of a university environment unsuited to the effects of their impairment (whether in terms of attendance or physical access) that most affected their learning.

Students generally preferred a mixture of teaching delivery methods but individual learning preferences were so diverse that the role of staff in being responsive to the needs of all students is all-important. However a major recommendation to emerge from this study (and already commonplace in guides to teaching and learning practice) is that lecture notes should be routinely provided in advance of lectures. While a desire by academic staff to maximise student attendance at taught class sessions is understandable, if notes are routinely made available after the lecture, it is difficult to see how a policy of non-provision in advance would make a significant difference to student attendance. One potential strategy is for staff to ensure that the 'added value' of lecture attendance is so great that it discourages students from using lecture notes as a substitute. However, this does raise issues of parity and fairness in relation to disabled students for whom impairment-related non-attendance is unavoidable. This dilemma illustrates the importance of staff flexibility towards diverse learner needs and preferences.

Disabled students clearly have more work to do around teaching and learning than their non-disabled peers. Being a disabled student involves additional planning and organisation that may be related to the effects of impairment, the provision of support, or actively managing disclosure and the reactions of others. Chapter 6 explores the implications of this 'emotional work' for disabled students in more detail. Students were commonly expected to be proactive in terms of informing staff about their impairment(s) and arranging their own reasonable adjustments. This is out of line with current Disability Discrimination legislation (see chapter 1), which requires that adjustments be anticipatory and not dependent on disclosure. In practice, fears about being perceived as 'different' to staff and their fellow students could prevent students from disclosing their impairment with the effect that reasonable adjustments to their learning were not put in place.

Institutional provision of reasonable adjustments to learning was extremely variable. Students were often not well informed about when they should disclose an impairment and about the support to which they were entitled, whether in the form of the DSA or other curricular adjustments. This lack of information could prevent students from being proactive about accessing reasonable adjustments, and from making fully informed decisions about how best to address their learning needs. Making decisions about the relative responsibilities of institutions to inform students about the support available and of students to be proactive about accessing reasonable adjustments is problematic but an issue that needs to be addressed by all higher education institutions. While appreciative of the support they received, students also raised considerable concerns about the inflexibility and unresponsiveness of disability support systems, particularly in relation to the DSA. It seems clear that there is potential for system efficiencies to be made by taking account of student preferences and being flexible, especially where unwanted equipment is being provided.

Staff attitudes were a crucial aspect of the teaching and learning experiences of disabled students. The characteristics of approachability, helpfulness, flexibility and being supportive, identified as most important by students, seem most likely to encourage disclosure by students of any impairment(s). While it can be very helpful for staff to be informed about the learning implications of particular impairments (some of which this chapter has highlighted), it is also important to recognise that the experience of impairment and its impact on learning can vary greatly between individuals.

Efforts to improve the teaching and learning experience of disabled students in higher education would be best concentrated on removing disabling barriers rather than making standardised adjustments based on impairment that do not take account of the diversity in students' learning needs and preferences. It is clear that flexibility is key when seeking to address these needs (and eliminate existing barriers) in terms of university support systems or staff attitudes to learning. In turn encouraging all students to articulate their individual learning needs, in the context of system-wide change that incorporates this diversity, can only be of benefit to the quality of teaching and learning practice within higher education.

Chapter 4

Assessing disabled students

Student and staff experiences of reasonable adjustments

Mary Fuller and Mick Healey

Context

This chapter focuses upon the experience and views of lecturing staff and disabled students of reasonable adjustments to assessment. It draws on successive interviews with 31 disabled students over the three-year period that students were undertaking their degree course. During the same period about 40 teaching sessions were observed and 50 of the staff who taught students in the longitudinal study were interviewed and asked specifically about issues arising for them and their institution in relation to reasonable adjustments and fair assessment. Interviews with the 31 students were informed by two surveys undertaken earlier at one of the participating universities. One survey consisted of questionnaire responses from 173 disabled students and four focus groups of 30 disabled students (Fuller, Bradley and Healey, 2004; Fuller *et al.*, 2004) prior to the enactment of the Special Educational Needs and Disability Act (SENDA). The second survey involved a different sample of 548 disabled and non-disabled students (Fuller, Hurst and Bradley, 2004) at the beginning of the research project in 2004 when the implications for universities of SENDA were still being considered and before we began interviewing disabled students and their lecturers.

Many writers claim that assessment 'is at the heart of the student experience' (Brown and Knight, 1994: 1), being the main driver of student learning in higher education:

> Assessment is a value-laden activity surrounded by debates about academic standards, preparing students for employment, measuring quality and providing incentives. There is substantial evidence that assessment, rather than teaching, has the major influence on

students' learning. It directs attention to what is important, acts as an incentive for study, and has a powerful effect on students' approaches to their work.

(Boud and Falchikov, 2007: Back cover)

Assessment is important for university staff, too, because of its calls on their time and its long-term impact on students:

Nothing that we do to, or for, our students is more important than our assessment of their work and the feedback we give them on it. The results of our assessment influence our students for the rest of their lives and careers – fine if we get it right, but unthinkable if we get it wrong.

(Race *et al.*, 2005: xi)

It is therefore unsurprising that both disabled students and the staff who taught them raised a variety of overlapping issues about assessment which are discussed in the rest of this chapter. Staff, who were specifically asked about feedback, had more to say about it than students where the topic was allowed to emerge spontaneously during interview. Underlying many staff comments were concerns with academic standards and preparing students for employment, the latter not restricted to the more obviously vocational courses. Students seemed less concerned about these two issues and more about consistency and fairness in the adjustments made to assessment.

Formative and summative assessment

There is a useful distinction to be drawn between formative assessment (assessment for learning) and summative assessment, explicitly referred to by Boud and Falchikov (2007) and implicitly by Race *et al.* (2005), earlier:

The essence of formative assessment is that undertaking the assessment constitutes a learning experience in its own right. Writing an essay or undertaking a class presentation, for example, can be valuable formative activities as a means of enhancing substantive knowledge as well as for developing research, communication, intellectual and organisational skills. In contrast, summative assessment is not traditionally regarded as having any intrinsic learning value. It is usually undertaken at the end of a period of learning in order to generate a grade that reflects the student's performance. The traditional unseen end of module examination is . . . a typical form of summative assessment.

(East, 2008)

While we encountered few examples of work set solely for formative purposes, students were offered formative feedback on summative tasks which Irons (2008: 7) designates 'feedforward'. An Education lecturer at University 1 highlighted the need to develop formative assignments that led into summative assessment:

We set an assignment and that is really the vehicle for the assessment. We are trying to distinguish assessment from assignment. Assignment I see as an activity which is part of the learning process, that there are opportunities for you to chew over your ideas with the staff. And I am just emailing a student back with some feedback from her ideas about planning lessons . . . It has a formative role and a summative role as well.

(Lecturer Allison)

Lecturer Day describes a three-tiered approach to assessment in Computing, including several mini assessments that students do weekly, that gives the work a formative function:

It is coursework, only with three components. I do three time-constrained tests, which does really test the concepts of the module. After [the lecture], we go to the lab [where] they get the worksheets. They are not formidable, hard questions . . . they are gentle ones, so they can do them and the build confidence. In the lab . . . if they have problems, they don't understand something, we are there to help. That actually gets collected and gets marked as well. And then, they have got a largish problem, which integrates what has been done in the module . . . they are doing [it] on their own, but they can ask for help again, for the process or something is not clear to them, etc. Time-constrained tests constitute 30 per cent of the overall mark. Worksheets 30 per cent, then the other big problem is 40 per cent.

(Lecturer Day)

A Humanities lecturer focused on formative possibilities even when dealing with a summative task. The session observed was at the end of the course and directly linked to the end of module assignment, which as the lecturer explains, was used as much as a teaching as an assessment tool:

> The whole idea of the assignment is the finale of the course. It's not there to test their knowledge it's another piece of a research work. I'm not interested in making sure that the course has been successful by testing their knowledge. I want to use the assignment to extend their knowledge and pull things together.
>
> (Lecturer Dudley)

He gave written comments in two sections: commentary on strengths and weaknesses of the work (feedback) followed by advice on how to improve for next time (feedforward). He saw this as a two-way process, encouraging students to give evaluations of the course which he used to make changes.

An education course (University 3) used feedback sheets which highlighted marking criteria:

> The feedback sheet has the criteria set out in grade bands, and we highlight them, to show what the criteria are. [Students] not only see the comment for the criteria on what they have scored, if they look at the same criteria in a higher band, they can see what they should have done to have got a higher grade, so it does both purposes: how well they've done and how they could have done better. And then we also do, just a snippet at the end that we type in, strengths of the assignment, and things they could have done better.
>
> (Lecturer Dennis)

As feedback was word processed it would be easy to make it available electronically for students who required their feedback in alternative formats, though none had yet asked.

Computing students at University 3 taking a group project module had plenty of opportunity to receive feedback throughout the year and received comprehensive written feedback on the assessment itself, including a grid which related their work to the assessment criteria:

> They get feedback in several forms, so they get the copy of the grid, and then there's a cover sheet, and we write on these, and then we might write inside, you know, at appropriate points as

well. So there are quite a lot of areas where we would do that. And we have more than one assessor, and so we have sheets which are used internally, where the assessors write on them, and then we gather those comments together to write on the front sheet.

(Lecturer Dover)

As another Computing lecturer pointed out, different students make different use of feedback:

Some of them respond really well to [feedback], I think it's something within our field they're becoming more used to, I think in a lot of modules in other fields, there's very little formative feedback, so they're not used to having it, so they don't know what to do with it when they've got it.

(Lecturer Dean)

Lecturer Dean thought lecturers would be open to providing feedback in alternative formats if asked though none had been so far. Another lecturer at University 3 mentioned that some students had notetakers who noted oral feedback while others had dictaphones to record lectures and advice given to them.

An English literature lecturer at University 1 spoke at length about feedback on the essay that was returned to students prior to the exam essay which accounted for 25 per cent of the overall mark:

I will write . . . quite lengthy comments both on particular points and then [an] overview of the whole thing . . . in the hope that this is seen as formative assessment.

(Lecturer Armitage)

He wanted to be as available as possible to students: he had an office hour but also encouraged them to email for appointments at another time if they needed to. He thought this offered plenty of opportunity to discuss course issues with him, which Anne, who was full of praise for this lecturer, confirmed. She indicated that feedback practices varied between courses, being generally better in English than in history.

Other students commented on feedback in positive and negative ways giving examples of strategies they adopted in relation to both formative and summative assessment that took into account their particular needs as a person with a specific impairment(s). For example,

Cassie, who had dyslexia and was studying at University 2, focused on strategic planning to overcome her known difficulties with writing: she found extended written work particularly difficult. She therefore adopted a strategy of gradually taking on longer assignments over the period of the degree, including an independent study in her second year which counted less towards her final degree classification so that she had acquired experience of longer pieces before taking on a library-based extended essay in final year which counted substantially to her degree classification.

At University 4 written feedback seemed to work well for most students though both Barry (who had dyslexia and an undeclared medical problem) and Billy (who had mobility difficulties) would have preferred verbal face-to-face feedback. For Bella being able to come to terms with verbal criticism was considered a key part of her performance course. Dalia, a wheelchair user at University 3, liked small tasks very regularly as she used feedback in planning subsequent assignments.

Students discussed and evaluated a variety of arrangements made for assessment during their course and for final assessment. Few students specifically spoke about assessment as an incentive for study; rather more indicated that particular types of formative assessment enabled them to think and act more effectively about how to tackle assessment tasks. They had trenchant criticisms of some adjustments made and were full of praise for others. Other chapters, notably chapters 3 and 8, foreground students' views on these issues, but it is interesting to note some examples of student experiences and attitudes that are not discussed there.

Karrie, who was studying modern foreign languages and had cerebral palsy, had got used to using scribes and readers and felt she had no problems with using them in exams except on one occasion where a scribe did not speak the language she was studying (Spanish) and so could not spell. This meant that she had to do the exam without the normal support.

Dermot (University 3) and Teresa (University 1) both had epilepsy and had received similar support – laptop, recording equipment, extra time in exams – but had contrasting attitudes to extra time for exams and assignments. Teresa considered that her condition merited time extensions for assignments: 'They should give me twice as long! I can't work for half the week so I should get twice as long' (Teresa). In contrast, Dermot had not needed to request extra time for assignments: 'I can request extra time due to my disability but I haven't as of yet, luckily' (Dermot). They took opposite views about exams where Teresa thought getting extra time would be unfair:

> They asked me whether I thought my disability affected my read-ing or whatever. I don't feel, I mean I am a slow reader but I don't feel at all that I should be given extra time, whereas international students don't. So that wouldn't be right.
>
> (Teresa)

In contrast, Dermot found extra time in exams very helpful, especially when he injured his hand and accepted this adjustment without criticism:

> The extra time did help a lot . . . having someone to write for me did help because I'm right handed and I broke my little right finger.
>
> (Dermot)

Assessment issues arising from student and staff interviews

Variety and flexibility in assessment

Staff volunteered opinions about variety in forms of assessment, both formative and summative. Here is a History lecturer from University 1:

> I also like that there are a variety of different assessment pro-cedures which allow some students to shine in some types of settings and others to shine in others . . . The way honours courses are conducted in the school . . . is a bit more circumscribed so I have been less satisfied with the assessment procedures there.
>
> (Lecturer Allwood)

Lecturer David commented favourably on two different forms of assessment, peer marking and making a CD-Rom. Peer marking had been very successful:

> The students do their tasks and then they sit down and mark each other's and I think that's been highly successful in disseminating good practice, but also developing their skills in being critical about ICT usage. That's been really, really interesting . . . and

they've all enjoyed it and . . . done it with real enthusiasm and real professionalism.

(Lecturer David)

While admiring colleagues' use of CD-Rom as a medium for presenting an assignment Lecturer David nevertheless considered his own undergraduate groups too large to consider using it himself:

In IT, people make a CD-Rom, an educational CD-Rom, and I think that's really interesting and different way of assessing the students. We've put in the presentation in year one professional studies, but everything [else] is pretty much based on writing and I would like to see more diversity in our assessment.

(Lecturer David)

Michelle and Anne who were studying Arts subjects at University 1 welcomed the flexibility in assessments in their first two years, but had encountered very little in their last two years. On the other hand a lecturer at the same university provided students with opportunities for setting their own questions in consultation with him, though few did:

I also actually give them the opportunity to devise their own questions if they want to . . . and I suggest they do so in consultation with me . . . but very few of them take it up.

(Lecturer Armitage)

Disabled students and staff described a range of adjustments made to assessment and expressed a wide spectrum of opinions about such changes. The two education departments in our study illustrate the range well. In the post-1992 university (University 3) this included a focus on reflexive practice with students writing three reviews in addition to their learning journal in one module. Students were expected to be actively involved in their own assessment, leading seminars to work on the review of a lead lecture. Presentations were negotiated with tutors: students could choose any area of teaching and learning in school. Students were encouraged to use a range of mediums for presentation:

They're encouraged to use a range, so it's not just them talking to you. So we might have role-play, we might have audience participation, we might have some presentation, so yes, I would see a range, with IT included.

(Lecturer David)

The Education department in the pre-1992 university (1) used oral presentations, group presentations which were assessed on some courses and only one 'traditional' exam in each year. Many staff also offered students the opportunity to discuss assignments before submitting them. There was much emphasis on group work which could be problematic for students who were deaf or hard of hearing especially when the group presentations were part of the formal assessments (as they were in Year 2) but seemed to suit students with dyslexia.

At University 4 the form of assessment (practical, performance, presentations, essays and journals) varied across the five courses included in our study, although there was little choice in the particular form for a particular assignment, beyond choosing subjects for essays. The main difference as far as the students were concerned was whether or not there were written examinations.

At one of the pre-1992 universities (University 1) there was a stark difference between the science subjects with a sense that physics retained traditional assessment, while other sciences were beginning to make increasing use of e-learning and e-assessment especially in relation to developing mainly formative assessments. Indeed, electronic methods can be particularly useful for assessment, cutting out tedious elements for staff who can concentrate on other duties. Equally, it is particularly well-suited to special adaptations for students with official records of impairment. For example, when a student logged onto an e-assessment programme with their matriculation number, this automatically triggered the special settings they required (e.g. large print; special screen adaptations; longer time). This method also meant support in exams could be provided in a more discreet way.

Architecture (at University 1) was flexible in terms of assessment: students could choose in what format they presented. For example in creating a model they could use computer modelling, make it in wood or draw it. Studio work, which was central to this subject, allowed genuine dialogue between staff and students about students' presentations.

Consistency and fairness

The most important themes about assessment emerging from interviews with the disabled students were consistency and fairness.

Fairness especially is a recurrent theme in disabled students' reflection on the university teaching and learning environment and in their expectations and experiences of reasonable adjustments and access to resources in general. Much of their experience has already been touched on in chapter 3 and will not be repeated.

Students commented on a lack of consistency of practice in making reasonable adjustments to assessment during a course or at its end. There was lack of consistency between lecturers in the same subject area, in students' experiences, between one year of study and another and, where they studied more than one, between subjects. This inconsistency meant some students were confused about their assignments and found it difficult to adopt appropriate strategies for work. They saw this inconsistency as the basis of a certain lack of fairness in their treatment as unlike non-disabled students they had to work out what they were entitled to. Additionally some disabled students (see Teresa, earlier, for example) viewed some of the reasonable adjustments offered to them as being potentially unfair to non-disabled students in general or to specific groups in particular.

One inconsistency noted by nearly all students at University 4 was that extra time was given for exams but not for assignments. Students underlined the extra stress they felt in meeting assessment deadlines and could not see the logic in prioritising exams over other assessed assignments. As a way of circumventing this difficulty Barry would obtain a GP's note or apply for extenuating circumstances: while these strategies got him the extra time he needed they also consumed his time.

Practice in relation to assessment was inconsistent in the subject that Brandon studied: his lecturers gave plenty of time for assignments to be submitted in the first instance and Brandon felt he could ask them for extra time as long as he did not do it too often. In other words this adjustment relied on sympathy from tutors and did not seem to be regarded as an entitlement.

Even when students encountered significant difficulties in their studies some demonstrated a generous sense of fairness. For example, following a family bereavement, Euan failed nine out of ten of his final exams including several of his core exams which meant he was not allowed to progress into the final honours year. He engaged in a lengthy and ultimately unsuccessful dialogue with the university to try to get reinstated. However, he thought the decision was based on fairness to all students and that perhaps the university could not take account of his special circumstances.

Anne described the main difference between support at school and university as university being less 'hands-on' and less flexible. She got a certain extension and beyond that she could get no extra. She reflected interestingly on this suggesting that it was entirely fair: 'I have just got to keep up as best I can. There are only so many allowances people can make. Otherwise it is not like I am doing the whole degree' (Anne).

Perceived limitations to making reasonable adjustments to assessment

Staff reflected on what they saw as limitations in making reasonable adjustments to assessment and on specific challenges in particular subjects. Difficulties related to integrity of courses, timing and being able to follow up with particular students when essays were marked anonymously (the latter mentioned by staff at two universities in contrasting subjects, community education and geography). Lecturer Dover pointed out the difficulty in arranging alternative assessment in a group project module, as the whole module was designed around the assessment. The module was compulsory for some students and she thought that there would be a case for finding an alternative project for disabled students who could not complete a group project for whatever reason. She had had students with hearing impairments and autistic spectrum disorder, the two impairments for which group work could potentially be a barrier, but had worked with them to ensure they could complete the group project without disadvantage.

As regards timing of feedback, one lecturer had four weeks to return student work according to the university's student charter: planning assessment points so that feedback could be returned before the next assessment was due could be difficult with a short teaching term and within a modular scheme. Lecturer Day's aim to return in-class work sheets for assessment within a week was made difficult as all students (which might include those disabled students who were used to having time extensions) were given an automatic 48-hour extension on assessment deadlines if they requested it.

In relation to specific challenges within a discipline a lecturer in Hispanic Studies reflected on an experience with disabled students who were hearing impaired or had speech difficulties which altered how an assessment task was presented:

One of the tests in the final exam is listening comprehension done from a tape recorder or a video. We had an issue with two people who couldn't really hear mechanically reproduced sounds but they were OK with voice and lip reading aloud. If there isn't such a problem in the group there is a part which is also videoed or recorded. But it always includes passages read to the student and having to make sure that they can see the facial movement, etc., since we had that problem. So I actually introduced that as a routine component.

(Lecturer Appleby)

Here is an example of a potential difficulty being turned into a creative solution that permanently alters the way in which a particular skill set is assessed: the changed assessment is in place for all students and is one of the very few examples in our study of an inclusive assessment (see below).

Having looked at the varying circumstances in the four universities in this study it will be useful to place the staff and student experiences in a wider context of discussions about reasonable adjustments. There are three main types of reasonable adjustment which can operate at the institutional, department, discipline, course/module or lecturer level and are described in more detail now.

Types of reasonable adjustment to assessment

Individual assimilation and individual arrangements

This kind of reasonable adjustment involves special arrangements being made for individual disabled students to help them cope with existing assessment practices. Common examples mentioned included extra time or a separate room in exams (for example, a science student with panic attacks was provided with a separate room to take her exam and the course organiser sat with her), being provided with a notetaker or the use of a computer. With written course work an example would be the use of a sticker placed on the work to indicate that a student has dyslexia so allowance could be made in the marking for poor spelling and structure.

Nationally individual assimilation is by far the most common approach and reflects that 'participation in education continues to be focused on fitting people into what is already available' (Stuart, 2002: 22). From our research we conclude that individual adjustments, far from being made in light of a student's specific needs and contrary to what the term 'individual adjustment' might imply, tend to be applied formulaically according to the student's impairment. Earle and Sharp (2000) writing before they were required to make anticipatory adjustments' noted that higher education institutions in the UK over-whelmingly made special provisions for the assessment of disabled students on an *ad hoc* basis: Robson's later work (2004), our own previous research (Fuller *et al.*, 2004; Fuller, Bradley and Healey, 2004; Fuller, Healey and Bradley, 2004) and the research discussed here suggest little has changed. Waterfield and colleagues cogently argue that:

> Across the UK the extensive use of 'special examination arrange-ments' for disabled students is reactive practice which is indicative of an assimilation culture; it forces students to adopt a disability identity, . . . and at a purely practical institutional level, is an *ad hoc* response with resource and equity implications that are neither desirable nor sustainable.
>
> (Waterfield *et al.*, 2006: 81)

Several other students in this study would agree that the special arrangements made them feel different in an unwelcome way:

> But they do put me in a separate room which kind of felt a bit odd . . . Because it's full on segregation . . . They are putting me in the freak room.
>
> (Teresa)

There are many examples in other chapters of adjustments made (to teaching and learning) for a particular student on the basis of impairment, some welcomed and some experienced as unhelpful. Chapters 3, 6 and 7 give vivid examples of the ways in which students in this study felt compelled to negotiate their way in and around disabled identities in order to gain access to adjustments in teaching and assessment, a process to which some were resigned and others hostile.

Alternative assessments and alternative arrangements

Where an individual student would be disadvantaged by the usual form of assessment by his or her impairment, an alternative arrangement is offered for example, a viva may be used to test the same learning outcomes as a written assessment. (Note, this isn't only offered to dyslexic students.) Consider examples of two students from different universities of alternative arrangements and substitute assessments that took account of the unpredictability in each student's circumstances. Both students felt secure that such arrangements would be made without fuss. Dionne had an unseen physical impairment; if her condition prevented her from taking an exam with other candidates the department would ensure a different assessment for her to be taken when she could. If Teresa needed to miss an exam because of the migraines which were a side effect of the medication she took for epilepsy, arrangements were put in place for her to rewrite her paper:

> [The Disability Office] have made arrangements for if I am ill [the department] will write another exam paper which is fantastic . . . well, if I had missed one last week then [the department] would have written another paper and I could have sat it as soon as they'd written it. So it would have been quite soon after.
>
> (Teresa)

Inclusive assessments and inclusive arrangements

Instead of trying to assimilate disabled students into the existing assessment system or providing alternative assessments just for disabled students, a more radical approach is to design the assessment system from the beginning to be inclusive of all students.

> In this case *all* students, not just those who are disabled, are provided with alternative assessments designed to test the same learning outcomes. Inclusive assessment removes the distinction between assessing disabled and non-disabled students. It is at the heart of universal design for learning which focuses on being usable by all students without the need for adaptation.
>
> (Burgstahler, 2001)

Providing alternative assessments which test the same learning outcomes for all students allows for diversity in learning styles among students and avoids singling out disabled students for special treatment. Earlier in this chapter we noted how a final assessment of listening comprehension was changed from a tape recorded one to a live speaker, initially as an individual adjustment and then retained as good practice for all future students (i.e. an inclusive arrangement). Waterfield *et al.* (2006) provide some excellent examples of inclusive assessments which they claim will better serve the majority of disabled students.

When inclusive reasonable adjustments are put in place they are provided for *all* students. One example of inclusive adjustments is to make alternative assessments designed to test the same learning outcomes available to all students. Another example is the provision of handouts before lectures. Chapter 3 describes how students from all four universities found being given lectures handouts in advance useful.

Despite some interesting examples referred to earlier in this chapter of lecturers trying to introduce an element of choice for students, generally in this study there was little evidence of any move towards adjustments in modes of assessment to allow students with a range of impairments to demonstrate the achievement of learning outcomes in different ways.

Inclusive adjustments correspond with our argument that disabled students should not be treated as a separate category of student. This approach also allows for diversity in learning styles among students and avoids (often visibly) singling out disabled students from their peers. Instead, an inclusive approach to reasonable adjustments removes the distinction between teaching and assessing disabled and non-disabled students. As Adams notes:

> With universal design approaches, the curriculum is flexible enough to meet the unique needs of the learner. With the increasing availability of powerful digital technologies, it is possible to create more flexible, or customised, learning environments for diverse learners. For me, the beauty of it is that an individual's impairment is not seen as a barrier but rather, the focus of how best that individual learns is the central concern.
>
> (2007: 9–10)

Earle and Sharp (2000) argue that most alternative assessments are compensatory in nature and do not test exactly the *same* skills and knowledge. According to them such assessments are 'inappropriate and misguided' being 'discriminatory and counter-productive' (Earle and Sharp, 2000: 541). On the other hand such practices may continue because inclusion is seen as recognising and providing for difference as captured in Elton's comment: 'I cannot think of anything more unfair than . . . to treat all students as if they are the same, when they so manifestly are not (2000: 1).'

Alternative and individual arrangements diverge from the spirit of the Disability Equality Duty if they are the only form of reasonable adjustment offered. While universities and colleges should not treat disabled students less favourably than their peers and the Disability Equality Duty requires them to make proactive system changes rather than individual reactive decisions, it has to be recognised that anticipatory reasonable adjustments may need to be supplemented with specific individual or alternative arrangements in certain cases and in particular circumstances.

While individual adjustments will always be necessary in certain cases (and we would argue these are a minority), inclusive practice in the provision of reasonable adjustments will remove the need for large numbers of often unwieldy individual adjustments.

Concluding thoughts

We infer from our research that there continues to be significant variation in practice regarding assessment: disabled students in our study encountered diverse policies and practices at institutional, departmental and individual lecturer level in *how* assessment was carried out, its *timing* and *what* was assessed. What they did not experience was an academic world in which there had been large-scale change towards more inclusive assessment practices. Another study of Scottish and English higher education institutions found that:

> Even within the same institution, lecturers often had only a hazy understanding of institutional policy on reasonable adjustments in assessment. For example, there was a lack of consistency within and between institutions with regard to making allowances for poor spelling or structuring.
>
> (Riddell *et al.*, 2005: 92)

So some of the differences that students experienced in relation to assessment may stem from uncertainty among both students and staff as to what reasonable adjustments are possible as well as inconsistencies in the application of institutional policies (see also chapter 9). The implications are stark:

> There has been ample evidence that without proper sets of

assessment adjustments which mirror the adjustments made to access the curriculum throughout the studies of disabled students, the examinations would inevitably measure not the academic achievement of disabled students but their disability.

(Konur, 2002: 146)

Compared to teaching, assessment practices have arguably been slower to change. Writing in relation to schools, Simpson (2005) has argued that assessment is regarded as a process which is largely separate from teaching and learning, requiring systems developed by technicians and measurement experts to judge accurately and reliably the learning outcomes achieved in relation to pre-determined knowledge or skills. Assessment remains focused on the learning achieved by the individual student, with little attention to the social context in which learning takes place. Similar arguments apply to higher education, where the standard forms of examination and written assignment have remained largely unchanged for many decades, despite an ongoing focus in development and research work on how to improve assessment technologies (Elton, 2004). Morley (2003) and Leathwood (2005) note that some attempts to modernise assessment in higher education, such as a new focus on student self-assessment and criterion-referenced assessment, which may have their roots in student empowerment narratives (Broadfoot, 1999), may in practice be experienced as new forms of regulation and surveillance by students and staff, and may do little to challenge structural inequalities in assessment systems.

Broadfoot (2002: 5) notes that 'any attempt to challenge the boundaries of conventional assessment is bound to provoke many new questions'. This may be the case especially where the challenge is seen as making special provision: 'Altering teaching and assessment approaches for particular students is likely to be far more contentious [than tackling physical barriers], since questions of fairness and the maintenance of academic standards inevitably arise' (Riddell et al., 2005: 78).

The higher education establishment has defended the need for clear qualification criteria based on disability status in order to determine which students should be entitled to alternative forms of assessment. The implications of enforcing a binary divide between disabled and non-disabled students are that universities continue to provide support for disabled students predominantly to those who disclose an impairment, who are thereby forced at some level to adopt a disabled identity to obtain the support for learning to which they are entitled. Universities in large part have avoided the more systemic change – anticipatory reasonable adjustments – that recent legislation implies and requires.

Assessment practice is patchy, but changing in some subjects, though in general it has not caught up with the notion of anticipatory adjustments. Wide variation in the experience of the students in the reasonable adjustments made indicate there are differences in how the legislation is interpreted, as shown in the diverse policies and practices of institutions, departments and individual tutors. Some of these differences point to cultural variations at institutional, department and discipline levels as to the appropriate ways to assess students as shown in various chapters in this book. It seems that approaches to teaching, learning and assessment in particular subject areas and institutions are based on deep-rooted understandings of what counts as valid knowledge, with associated assumptions about appropriate ways to convey that knowledge and test whether learning has taken place. For change to take place, these fundamental constructs must be challenged.

Chapter 5

Curriculum and pedagogy

Challenges and dilemmas for teaching staff

Alan Hurst

Introduction

Since 1990 policies on increasing the participation rates of disabled students have been successful in terms of recruitment although statistics hide inconsistencies between courses and programmes within universities and also between universities. Because of this relative success, attention has shifted to the quality of students' educational experiences. This chapter explores the nature of the challenges in learning and teaching identified by staff and students. It considers five broad groupings of challenges and dilemmas: the nature of the subject and the design of the curriculum, the chosen methods of teaching and learning, the particular specific institutional context, personal dimensions, and the four Ds (defining disability, the Disability Discrimination Act [DDA], disclosure and dyslexia).

Curriculum design

Recently more attention has been given to universal course design and the ways in which adopting this approach from the start should increase accessibility and minimise the need for reasonable adjustments required by the anti-discrimination law. It is also a way of meeting anticipatory duties, the other legal requirement. Because this approach to course design has only gathered momentum in recent years, the experiences of the students and staff in this research project pre-date such developments and changes which might have ensued.

It is possible to identify six topics of concern from the data collected in the investigation:

Content of courses

Staff might become more familiar with aspects of disability if it were included within the curriculum of as many subjects and courses as possible. For example, at University 1 architecture students were taught about making buildings accessible to comply with disability legislation. There is scope to promote this on a greater scale.

Flexibility of courses

Anne started a degree in English. At the end of the second year when she had to decide whether to go for single honours, she chose joint honours in English and History. Her main concern was the quantity of written work – her new programme did not involve a long dissertation. It also meant:

> A greater choice [of modules] . . . Because I am doing joint honours I get to put my own course together . . . I have got some really exciting courses in English coming up.
>
> (Anne)

Requirements of professional bodies and fitness to practise

Arguably the clearest example relating entry to professions and fitness to practise involves initial teacher training courses. One lecturer said:

> There was some discussion about things, I remember, to do with admissions, under what circumstances was it permissible to reject somebody because they weren't going to be able to complete the course and meet the requirements for Qualified Teacher Status and if you did it this way, that was OK but if you did this way it was in conflict with the disability legislation.
>
> (Lecturer Dawson)

Maintaining standards

Some staff expressed a concern for standards and whether some disabled students are able to meet them. Chapter 2 discusses the debate about maintaining academic standards in more detail. One lecturer commented:

Just one or two people who have been accepted in previous years, because they were disabled almost. They just couldn't cope. They were absolutely set up for failure. Because you can't set up different standards and we are quite good at not doing that.

(Lecturer Ashcroft)

Electronic-based learning

Most universities have developed e-learning policies and provision using a range of approaches and technology. In interviews there were often references to WebCT. One tutor observed that these developments were not made with the needs of disabled students in mind:

Not specifically for disabled students that spring to mind. It may be a by-product of some changes. And I know that some courses . . . have a lot of WebCT-based exercises which are being developed . . . and some of these may be easier for disabled students to handle, they can take their time doing it.

(Lecturer Allen)

Some departments are less advanced than others:

At the moment we are one of the departments that are not good at WebCT but part of this project is to make us better at WebCT. We will get round to WebCT and I think it is good – particularly we want to get into it because we run two courses . . . Chemistry with a year in Europe and Chemistry with a year in industry.

(Lecturer Ashwood)

Learning and teaching

Chapter 3 considers the experience of students participating in the project in relation to learning and teaching in detail. The source of most comment was the provision of lecture notes in advance of classroom sessions. This is frequently seen as a simple 'reasonable adjustment' for disabled students. Views on this from both staff and students varied:

If I am using any kind of overheads . . . I always put my material [online] after the session. I appreciate that there is an argument for putting it on before the session. You start to wonder what the point of them actually going and standing and giving the lecture is if you just give the students the script in advance.

(Lecturer Abercromby)

I suppose I don't really agree with lecture notes in advance in the sense that it encourages people not to go. If they freely got the lecture notes available then they won't turn up . . . and you hear people . . . saying to you 'how many have you missed this block?' You know 'I can miss another two and I won't get any marks taken off.' And I am thinking that's just the wrong attitude really.

(Karrie)

They put slides up during the lectures and you try and write down what is on there and they become available on the Internet a couple of days later. Other lecturers would put them on the Internet a couple of days before the lecture so you could print them off and have what they were going to say and annotate that and you could get much more information written down.

(James)

Many staff use PowerPoint presentations in their classrooms, but some have concerns about it as a medium for teaching:

And I worry about PowerPoint because we only use that and we have had some serious discussions in the department and school and professional training on the use of PowerPoint. I read some research undertaken in another HEI where they talk about PowerPoint being over-used now and it just makes dull, passive students.

(Lecturer Davidson)

While Daisy finds lecture notes helpful she does not like PowerPoint handouts:

What I sometimes find annoying is if they give you a PowerPoint handout with the bits you can write on next to it and they do something like a class that is totally on the board and you have to write it in or 'arhhhh how does that work?' As long as the note-taker's there then it's all good; if they're not there for some reason and you're on your own then it can be a bit of a nightmare.

(Daisy)

The concerns expressed by staff lead to questions about the effectiveness of lectures as a teaching strategy. Lecturer Davidson, who likes to make her teaching sessions as interactive as possible, is a case in point. She does not consider large lectures to be good learning environments:

> I do try to make it as highly interactive as I can and with a big group that's obviously difficult. What I try and do is have a mixture of me talking, video analysis, discussion in pairs, feedback as a group. So, I try to put in everything, so that the students don't rely, well, firstly that students aren't just sat there for an hour listening to me, but also that students are engaging in the listening process.
>
> (Lecturer Davidson)

Cara gives an example of a lecturer who breaks up his lectures in recognition that students find it difficult to concentrate throughout lectures:

> He always says that he's sick of seeing his students falling asleep in the middle of lectures, so he does like 20–25 minutes of the lecture and then he stops the lecture and makes everybody get up and dib ... we have a little key thing and there's a machine at the front where you have to dib it in and record your attendance, if you're there or not. Most lecturers do it at the beginning, you dib as you walk in. He does it halfway through the lecture because he says you're not going to concentrate for 50 minutes.
>
> (Cara)

There was some consensus between staff and students in what they regarded as 'good teaching' and 'bad teaching'. Regarding his teaching session, which had been observed for this research, one lecturer says:

> One of the things that I like to think is the key to good teaching is that you try to accommodate all the preferred ways of learning. There was some chat, some talk about key ideas, there was substantial consideration and exploration of that in the music making and then from that drawing the key idea. I did use my board. I am aware all the time that some people like pictures and some like

words and some people like sounds. And therefore I know in the balance of my two hours of time that I have something for everybody!

(Lecturer Aitchison)

Asked to identify a teaching setting in which he did not feel well supported, Duncan gave an example where he felt there was insufficient guidance around an assignment and the feedback was too vague:

They haven't really given us a focus of what the assignment's supposed to be on. They've just sort of said: '[you] need to write a 3,000-word essay, pick a title, go and do it'. They haven't given us titles or anything. They did give us a mock up, sort of start thing a couple of weeks back but the feedback on it was very generic, it was very, 'this is too general, this needs to be more specific', sort of thing. There wasn't any; 'you need to change that for that and you need to go into more detail on this'. So that's sort of a harder one to do.

(Duncan)

While flexibility can be an advantage to disabled students, this example shows that there is also a need for it to be accompanied by appropriate guidance.

The institutional context

Internal organisation and administrative structures

The four universities in this study have all developed different internal structures and systems including those for supporting disabled students (see chapters 1 and 9). Some of these appear to be more helpful than others. For example, while all had a well-established central service for this group of students, the links between these and individual academic departments/faculties varied. In University 4, all faculties, academic departments and services had a named contact. Communication between these individuals was frequent and regular, covering a variety of matters. Other universities did not have such a clear structure:

We have to do certain things and this department relies heavily on

the Disability Office to tell us what we are going to do then we do
it. So if they want to put a recorder in front of the lecture theatre
that is fine, if they want a video, fine . . .

(Lecturer Ashwood)

Another lecturer suggests that moving towards more devolved responsibilities might be appropriate:

> I think probably, well I don't know, we've got the disability advisor,
> which is obviously a very good central point and I was just won-
> dering to what extent, if we had a named person in the school
> of education who was responsible for the disabled students, so
> there was somebody who linked with the disability advisor. So,
> you know like a SENCO [special educational needs co-ordinator]
> in school, there was a SENCO here who had their finger on the
> button.

(Lecturer Davidson)

Effective support and positive comments from students were associated
with the size of departments. A student said:

> We're quite close in this department on the whole and there's a
> lot of inter-relationships – it's a very friendly department. We
> are very friendly with the tutors. And I feel privileged, very, very
> privileged in that way.

(Rebecca)

Many students commented on differences not only between departments but also between staff in the same department. In relation to the
former, student Jean says:

> The [subject] lecturer, I had him right at the beginning of the
> block. He was excellent. He was very much, it was very much
> discovering . . . you go off and do this and I felt very cosseted by
> him all the way through . . . I was quite emotional because I was
> thinking am I [dyslexic] or not and there was all these [dyslexia
> diagnosis] tests going on . . . I was quite upset by the whole feel-
> ing. But he was very much mix in, get to know people and support,
> he was excellent.

(Jean)

Physical environment

Each higher education institution (HEI) is located in a different local environment. Their sites present a range of building styles, open spaces and overall layout. The result is that there are considerable variations in their accessibility to disabled students. When there is discussion of the physical environment, the focus turns immediately to the challenges posed for those with impaired mobility. However, it must not be forgotten that university sites might also be made more accessible and user-friendly to people with auditory and visual impairments. Accessibility is more than the installation of ramps, elevators and accessible rest rooms. Some comments from lecturers suggest that they are aware of this:

> It is a more accessible lecture theatre but it's actually a really horrible lecture theatre to give lectures in . . . it's the acoustics, it's the atmosphere . . . There is no natural light . . . It looks like a Stalinist torture chamber; it feels like a Stalinist torture chamber!
> (Lecturer Armitage)

Health and safety

Even before the greater attention paid to health and safety issues in recent years, it was sometimes used as a first excuse rather than as a last resort to prevent disabled students being accepted on to a course. Under the terms of the anti-discrimination law it is a valid reason to turn down an application from a disabled person but this should occur only after a thorough exploration of possible reasonable adjustments. In one university the safe emergency evacuation of students who use wheelchairs had become the responsibility of university staff rather than the fire services. This led to a new policy where mobility-impaired students were not allowed into rooms above ground level.

Setting priorities

Working to support disabled students is low status work. Most universities have other, higher priorities. This attitude transfers to the staff and can be seen in comments such as:

> We work in a research-intensive university which is RAE [Research Assessment Exercise] driven. And if you ask staff to spend a lot of

time getting materials ready for a handful of students, whereas they could be doing research then that is difficult to manage . . . Certainly in this school, I would suspect within this university, I would say it is the biggest challenge.

(Lecturer Ashwood)

Approaches to staff training and continuing professional development

It is evident already that many of the challenges could arise from a lack of training. For example, Cassie states:

They can't teach. They're very knowledgeable but they're rubbish at getting the point across and they can't teach . . . there's one lecturer last year, who was dreadful and the reading list he gave us was practically all his books, so, even if you went to the reading list to try and understand it better . . . But, no he was, I mean he was very knowledgeable, a very good Professor blah, blah, blah but he just couldn't teach. And his academic style was very complicated, because the textbooks were just impossible to read.

(Cassie)

There are two dimensions to this: basic training for life as a teacher in an HEI, and specialist training about disability and staff responsibilities following changes to the law.

In the past 20 years slow progress has been made in providing basic training in teaching in higher education for inexperienced staff. In one department only one member of staff had completed the Postgraduate Certificate in Higher Education (PGCHE), as the rest of the staff joined the department long before this was a requirement. The staff member who completed the PGCHE found it very useful in developing his teaching practice. Supporting disabled students was the exclusive focus of one of the teaching sessions and was covered extensively in three others. Another lecturer had originally qualified as a secondary school teacher and found that this qualification and experience were relevant to teaching university-level students. A third lecturer gained membership of the Higher Education Academy, through the experiential route. She was also a member of the steering group that established the original postgraduate teaching qualification at the university and monitored the course through its formative years. She has attended numerous workshops and training sessions focused on teaching practice throughout her career and maintains a keen interest in pedagogy.

There are issues associated with the provision of training (Hurst, 2006). It seems as if the following lecturer is seeking simple easy-to-apply solutions to what are often different and complex circumstances:

> My only slight qualm about these sort of things is that I feel you don't really get sufficient information about how to present things, you know? Sometimes it's nice to have a set of recommendations or guidelines that say 'do this', 'use this', do it this way and this will work'. And not just for dyslexia, but for partially sighted, deaf people, whatever. A lot of these things tend to be, 'get into groups and discuss this among yourselves and see what you can come up with'. Well, that's fine, but at the end it would be nice sometimes to have some outside expert coming in and saying this will work, you can do this, you can do that, we don't seem to get enough of that I don't think.
>
> (Lecturer Darton)

Others find the training valuable and that it helps them develop:

> I don't know about how it changes the way I teach, because I still do things the same, I still plan what I'm going to teach, I still have objectives, for a session, I still get to the end and think, did I achieve what I wanted to, so that's no different to children . . . So the PGCHE bit of it has just made me look a bit more at how older people learn, as opposed to how children learn . . . so reading up the stuff, ready for the report I've got to do, and it's just giving me more background on the theory of that.
>
> (Lecturer Dennis)

A major issue is whether sessions which educate staff about disability should be compulsory. In at least one HEI there was a compulsory staff training day run by the institution to familiarise staff with the requirements for higher education as laid out in the Special Educational Needs and Disability Act (SENDA). Of the three lecturers interviewed who attended this, only one can remember specifics of what was discussed during the training:

> It wasn't enough detail. I think it was more covering the sort of requirements of the legislation and saying from this date you

will have to do this and this, but not exactly what a reasonable accommodation might be. So I think their training probably includes a few examples of what a reasonable accommodation might be, but not sufficient to enable everybody to work out how their courses or assessments might need to be changed.

(Lecturer Dawson)

Individual and personal factors

Knowledge of impairments and their potential impact on study

Given the level of general ignorance about disability in contemporary society, it should come as no surprise that there were considerable variations in the knowledge that staff had about the range of impairments. For example, some might need to be reminded of the distinction between visible and invisible impairments. Cara was concerned about the lack of support from her department, particularly as a bout of depression has the potential to have knock-on effects:

> And that's why if the work gets too much, or I keep starting to get bad grades, when I know I've put the effort in and I know all the knowledge is in it, and I knew what I wanted to write but I'd get a bad mark back, that sort of hampers down on that side as well, so it kind of, the two kind of conflict with each other . . . So sometimes it would be nice if I can say, look, back off a minute, because otherwise it could make me very ill, in terms of, makes me run down anyway, because I was, I always seem to have to spend more time than anyone else doing work.
>
> (Cara)

Lack of knowledge of assistive technology and reasonable adjustments

It would be inappropriate to expect lecturers to be fully aware of the ways in which assistive technology has developed to support disabled students. However, there are some basic points with which they should be familiar. For example, changing the presentation of print-based materials can be helpful in making them more accessible to some students. Cassie would benefit if handouts were provided on coloured paper:

Well, the lecture notes could come in coloured rather than in black and white but then when I print it out, I print it out on coloured paper anyway. I don't know really, I think maybe, I think the lecturers should make a bit more of an effort, like put links to different websites or different materials, I mean they don't have to do something every week but just something a bit more.

(Cassie)

Lack of prior experience of working with students with a particular impairment

If asked about the challenges they face when including disabled students in their classes, some staff comment on their lack of prior experience. One lecturer finds it difficult to pinpoint the greatest challenge in teaching disabled students. He feels that he has had limited experience and even in the case of dyslexic students the difficulties have not seemed too great. However, he does worry that this suggests that he is insensitive to the difficulties faced by these students and also that he is not responding fully:

My experience has been quite limited . . . to students with dyslexia . . . And maybe this was just my insensitivity . . . but there didn't seem to be really that much difficulty in them having a kind of full learning experience . . . I am not really sure . . . I can't really think of anything.

(Lecturer Armitage)

Lack of time

Making effective provision for disabled students is often viewed as time-consuming, an additional demand coming when teaching staff are faced with many others, often seen as having greater priority. Students recognised this:

Tutors are extremely busy and when you can't find the tutor it goes to the next day and you phone and leave a message but he doesn't get back to you – I realise it's his workload that stops him being available.

(Barry)

One lecturer cited lack of time as the reason for not participating in staff development:

> I don't have time. That is not a sort of parting comment. That is a real aspect of the context. You can offer things endlessly, if people are not in a position to take it up then it is not going to get taken up. I would like to be given more time, more space for people to become more informed and develop their own ideas. It isn't just about getting information. It is about developing you ideas so that these things can enhance your teaching. And I really do think that the anti-discrimination agenda can really enhance our teaching. It isn't just about making the demands . . . but we need more resources.
>
> (Lecturer Ashcroft)

Continuing challenges and dilemmas for teaching staff: the four Ds

Based on research conducted in this study there were four additional concerns for staff: definitions of disability, DDA, disclosure and dyslexia.

Definitions and models of disability

The underpinning issue about how disability is defined is associated in particular with impairments that are not immediately visible and sometimes impact intermittently on the individual. Simple examples are epilepsy and ME. An issue of concern for one academic is the difference between disability and illness. It arose because of the condition of a particular student and he raised it with the university, but got no response:

> I asked the university to advise me on the distinction between a disabling condition like Crohn's disease and illness. . . . if a student misses the exam because they are ill then the university policy is that they take a resit examination in the next diet . . . the university hasn't really replied to me. The student was diagnosed with Crohn's disease . . . newly diagnosed . . . she had a problem with medication and so on, so missed the June exam diet . . . then missed them in August as well for the same reason . . . I was arguing that she wasn't ill but that she was disabled and the university

had a responsibility to deal with her in a different way . . . and therefore find a way that she was allowed to pass these courses.

(Lecturer Allen)

In pursuing the requirements of the law and in trying to make learning and teaching more inclusive, there is the implicit application of a social model of disability. One lecturer demonstrated significant knowledge of models of disability and their implications:

It is something we have struggled with over the time that I have been here. I think there is a strong sense of commitment to that kind of . . . the idea of inclusion, particularly in relation to people with disabilities. One thing that we have found, although if you like theoretically and ideologically, we would probably, almost as one person say we are committed to the ideas of a social model of disability rather than a medical model of disability.

(Lecturer Abercromby)

Dyslexia

Many students and staff commented on several issues relating to dyslexia although it is interesting to note that the majority tended to see it as a form of specific learning difficulty (i.e. the application of an individual/medical deficit model of disability) rather than a learning difference.

It is clear that there is some lack of knowledge about the impact of dyslexia on study patterns. One academic saw it narrowly in terms of the ability to spell correctly:

You have to be careful that you don't get cynical because in these big classes you get ten scripts or so or more, which are dyslexic. And, well, there are some students where you don't really see it. They are just normal scripts; you can't find any mis-spellings, not more than any other student.

(Lecturer Alexander)

In contrast, Jean was given encouraging support while on an Initial Teacher Training course, a programme which is sometimes difficult for students with dyslexia to join:

I knew she was doing them because of me but she never ever made a fuss. Like simple things, if she put an overhead up in a lecture theatre, or even a workshop, I found it hard to keep my place and I can't actually follow it on a piece of paper . . . she would either take another blank piece of paper, turn it over and lay it down and, either do paragraph by paragraph, or line by line it if was a really difficult font.

(Jean)

The difficulties facing students wishing to have careers in school teaching are shown in interviews with academics:

I find it hard to see how people with severe dyslexia could be teachers, simply because they're modelling language for children, and if they have trouble with it themselves, how could they do it for children? Every time they prepare something for children to look at, how do you know it's going to be accurate? So children might be picking up the mistakes that that person makes, so that's an issue.

(Lecturer Dennis)

In the face of comments such as this, from the point of view of the student it raises the important issue of whether to tell the university or work placement that they are dyslexic or have other impairments. Chapter 6 discusses the dilemmas involved for two Initial Teacher Training students, Jean and Andrew, in more detail.

Disclosure

The significance of disclosure for entry to some professions is evident from recent investigations by the Disability Rights Commission. Studies looked at the issue of disclosure of unseen impairments by staff employed in nursing, social work and school teaching (Lin *et al.*, 2006; Stanley, Ridley *et al.*, 2007). Disclosure is a cause of concern for students because they feel it might lead to discrimination of some kind (see chapter 7 for more on the dilemmas of disclosure). Once the information has been made known, there are additional concerns about confidentiality; for example Cara was concerned about whether worries about confidentiality were actually preventing staff from making the adjustments necessary to support her (see chapter 3).

For members of the teaching staff, the issue is about getting the information in advance so that there is sufficient time to plan the required adjustments:

Well, [notification from Disability Office] has been a particular
difficulty. And I think in a way it has raised some issues. In the
past there was conflict between disclosure and confidentiality.
But I think the DO erred on the side of confidentiality. And this
made it difficult for people to go forward for the disabilities act
because they didn't know . . . how far we could disseminate information that was on the one hand confidential but on the other
hand [needed for] action by a diverse set of people. I think the
DO has moved to a much more pragmatic approach and 'need to
know' basis of disclosure

(Lecturer Allen)

Once an institution is made aware of a student's impairment, the legislation requires it to make reasonable adjustments. However, if a student chooses not to disclose it would be difficult for them to allege
discrimination subsequently if their needs had not been met. Hence it
is important that all staff know the legal position, in particular SENDA
2001 and the more recent DDA 2005.

DDA

There are two matters to note in relation to legislation. Firstly, if teaching staff make blanket assertions of the kind made by this Chemistry
lecturer they allow for the possibility of legal action to be taken against
them:

You can't do Chemistry if you have got a sight impairment. You
can't do it . . . they have just never done Chemistry at school.

(Lecturer Ashwood)

If this position is adopted and becomes inflexible there is a risk
of action under the anti-discrimination law. To avoid this and to
strengthen their position if challenged about refusing to offer places,
staff need to identify the core non-negotiable parts of the study programme and to show that even with reasonable adjustments it would
be impossible for a student with a particular impairment to meet them.

Secondly, whilst policy regarding staff training was mentioned earlier, it is interesting to note that some lecturers showed concern about
their changed situation following the implementation of the anti-
discrimination law. Lecturer Dennis feels that he and his colleagues
can easily assume that, as no one has complained, everything must be

ok, but he recognises this might not be the case and would not necessarily know what to do if someone did complain:

> Perhaps there's an argument for a little session on what happens if we get it wrong, and students complain, you know, what could be the outcomes if somebody took us through the wash over it . . . because I think some of us just, sort of, blissfully carry on and think we're doing ok, but if somebody came up and said 'well actually, I'm entitled to this, and they haven't provided it', what would be the, you know, the burden on the university for that, and that might just sharpen people up a bit, as to what they're doing.
>
> (Lecturer Dennis)

More extreme is the view of the recently appointed Lecturer Armstrong, with a background in special education, who considered discussion at University 1 about disability to be five years behind the times (see chapter 6).

A third lecturer felt that the institution was trying to pass on institutional responsibilities to individual members of staff and doing so without recognising any additional implications such as costs:

> To be honest I have no idea [how the institution has responded]. My impression is that, like so much else in the institution and elsewhere, is that responsibility is being pushed down . . . And I think that DDA is expected to be delivered at ground level without any more commitment. I think if you are serious about inclusion and that kind of thing it is very expensive.
>
> (Lecturer Ashcroft)

In terms of the two specifics of the SENDA, there is evidence already that students and staff have become aware of the need to put in place reasonable adjustments. What this study shows is that universities are currently less successful in implementing their anticipatory duties which should ensure things are in place prior to the arrival of the students and before their course begins.

Summary

Considerable progress has been made in developing policy and provision for disabled students in higher education including the classroom experience. On the other hand, it would be foolish to become complacent. There are still considerable challenges to overcome. This involves trying to change deep-seated and enduring cultures at many levels in the HEI, a process that is seldom straightforward and often meets resistance. We are still a long way from finding an HEI which can claim quite justifiably to be a genuinely inclusive place which meets the diverse range of students' needs in all of its routine policies, procedures and practices. When this stage has been reached, disability services will be seen as value-added provision rather than an additional institutional expense.

Chapter 6

Identity work

Ways of being a disabled student in higher education

Hazel Roberts, Jan Georgeson and Katie Kelly

Analysis of student identity can make an important contribution to understanding the different ways that students respond to the challenges and opportunities at university. Students classified as having the same disability according to their institution's system of categories had different, and sometimes contrasting, responses to the same reasonable adjustment or special provision. For example, we heard that some were delighted to receive laptop computers and dictaphones and considered them essential tools for study; others regarded them as, at best luxuries, or at worst an embarrassment.

At an early stage in the project it became apparent that much of what students told us about teaching and learning was underpinned by the complex and changing ways in which they positioned themselves in relation to disability. This prompted us to develop questions to shed light on how they felt about taking on the label of disabled student and the extent to which their impairment influenced how they felt about themselves as learners. This chapter has been developed from the responses students gave as they moved through university and as their understanding of themselves and their impairment changed. Common themes emerging from their accounts have been used to provide a framework to highlight key findings, but initially relevant literature on identity and disability, including the experience of university students, will be considered.

Identity and disability

The starting point for many theorists of disability is Hall's (1996) conception of anti-essentialist (or pluralist) identities. Hall questions the essentialist notion of identity as fixed and unchanging, based upon irreducible, natural characteristics that remain with the individual throughout life. Instead, he argues that identity is flexible and evolves over time, and that an individual acts out multiple identities.

Watson (2002: 511) using the work of Giddens (1991) argues for a pluralist understanding of identity for both disabled people and non-disabled people: 'our sense of self is constantly evolving. We constantly reconfigure ourselves through multiple identities, and time, space and relationality are all important in identity formation'. Disability is still a valid identity category, but 'such a classification must be historically situated, socially composite and seen as part of a multiple identity' (Watson, 2002: 513). Therefore identities must be seen as contingent and situational, and disability might be only one facet of conception of self.

Watson also advocates challenging existing narratives about disabled people which are underpinned by two key models of disability, the medical and the social. The medical model views impairment of some part of the body (or mind) as the direct cause of disability. The appropriate response to disability is seen as medical treatment and/or rehabilitation that seeks to make the disabled person as 'normal' as possible. The medical model is dominant in western accounts of disability, and seen by social model theorists as the main cause of the discriminatory social attitudes and institutional practices experienced by disabled people (Oliver, 1990; Tregaskis, 2002). This dominance is reflected in the universities in our study. The provisions of the Disability Discrimination Act (DDA) form the core of statutory requirements for university disability policies, but it can be criticised for its focus on the limitations of the individual, rather than considering societal barriers to carrying out 'day to day activities'. To access support, university students must 'fit' themselves into or identify themselves within a category system (e.g. dyslexia, visual impairment, epilepsy) that has roots in the medical model:

> In Higher Education, categories of impairment . . . serve the function of underlining the difference and separateness of disabled students from others and impose a view of impairment as an individual deficit rather than a structural problem, with the onus on the individual to accommodate to the institution rather than vice versa.
>
> (Riddell, 1998: 211)

Students arriving at university are therefore faced with seeking support through a process of self-categorisation which is then externally validated through assessment. This places the emphasis on themselves as needy recipients of pre-specified intervention rather than as agentive actors customising support to fit their needs from the array of reasonable adjustments available.

In contrast to this focus on the individual, the social model of disability focuses upon the structural problems inherent within society, including universities. Disability is viewed as a social construction, and as a form of oppression for people who have impairments. Society is the cause of disability, not individual impairments, and the 'cure' for disability is for society to alter its intrinsically disabling practices (Oliver, 1990; 1996). This model with its focus upon societal barriers is becoming increasingly acknowledged within the higher education environment: it places the onus on the institution to adapt and change disabling practices which form barriers to accessing services.

However, Watson (2002) questions the usefulness of both models as part of disabled identity. He interviewed disabled men and disabled women and found that impairment, the basis of the 'difference' of disabled people for both models, was not seen as important for their sense of self. While they recognised that they were different from 'non-disabled' people, this difference was not internalised as being central to identity, and some participants questioned the very meaning of normality. Watson argues that his participants are trying to access a 'mainstream identity', through minimising the importance of their impairments.

We concur that the medical versus social model debate is unhelpful and polarising when considering the construction of disabled students' identity. The debate considers the construction of disability from an external position that does not adequately consider the lived experience of individuals or their agency in seeking to alter or reject the tenets of these models. The models can be seen instead as narratives that may influence but do not determine identity formation, and which disabled people might call on when accounting to others for any special treatment or 'difference'. So the term 'disabled person' might be politically or socially useful to access services or legitimise extra resources, but not necessarily be rooted in the lived experience of individuals, which is what this chapter seeks to document.

Being – or feeling – different from other people can depend on what kinds of difference are recognised, valued or minimised within the different contexts in which an individual is involved. We learn about who we are in the everyday interactions and activities of the social groups to which we belong. We learn this through other people's responses to what we do and say, and reify this learning when we talk about ourselves:

> People tell others who they are, but even more important, they tell themselves and then try to act as though they are who they say they are. These self-understandings, especially those with strong emotional resonance for the teller, are what we refer to as identities.
>
> (Holland *et al.*, 1998: 3)

The students in our study arrived at university with their own personal histories of impairment. Some had a strong sense of their particular needs and the confidence and inclination to see that these needs were met. For others, only at university did they find themselves classified as disabled or feel comfortable with being different and because of this were just beginning to understand how to ensure that their needs were met. Often the development of their different understandings of their own impairment and different response to the demands of university life could be attributed to the ethos or culture of their varying prior educational or work experiences.

Olney and Brockelman (2003) demonstrate how disabled students seek to reject medical model stereotypes of the experience of disability. Students themselves reframe the debate so that their understanding of identity cannot be captured by a binary medical model/social model distinction. These authors also document the sophisticated interpersonal skills that disabled university students develop during the complex process described by Low (1996; see below) as 'identity negotiation'. They found that students' sense of identity was context dependent and that disclosure of impairment was often managed on a 'need to know' basis, fitting with the pluralist view of identity as contextual and temporal.

Low (1996: 242) sees disabled university students as primarily seeking to negotiate a non-disabled identity in order to be seen as a 'normal' student. Students with visible disabilities frequently make efforts to conceal them and people with concealable disabilities often work to keep them hidden. However, paradoxically, within a university setting students are also required to assume a disabled identity in order to access services. The tactics of negotiation include: 'speaking out and increasing visibility, reasoning with others, using humour, adopting aggressive or assertive attitudes, avoiding confrontation with others and distancing themselves from other students with disabilities' (Low, 1996: 244).

Christie *et al.* (2008) highlight the emotional risks involved in assuming a student identity for all students, but particularly those from non-traditional backgrounds, while Goode (2007) emphasises the emotional work done by disabled students on their own behalf and on behalf of others. In Goode's study, students' judgements about the degree of emotional work necessary to obtain their rights could affect how proactive they were about accessing teaching and learning. Students seeking support can become 'extra visible' in a negative way while others (such as those with physical impairments) can be automatically 'visible'. This could raise tensions as Goode agrees with Low (1996) that students' primary goal in relation to their identity is to negotiate a non-disabled identity.

Student voices

Project participants were a self-selected subset of disabled students at each university. Therefore they had all in some context declared an impairment to the university although, as we shall see, this did not necessarily imply that disability was a part of their self-identity. We asked students primarily about disability in terms of their sense of identity and their identity as a disabled student, which may have led to students attributing a greater role to disability in their identity formation than if asked about their identity generally. However, participation in a longitudinal project of this kind might also have given a context for students to reflect on their personal processes of identity formation and to make sense of their own experiences throughout their university career.

Many students in this study did not consider the disability category ascribed to them by their institution relevant to their sense of self. With this in mind, we have not sought to emphasise these categories within the student accounts. However, Appendix A.1 provides further information about students in the study including their impairment(s).

Major themes

Students and models of disability

The project findings lead us to argue that the medical and social models of disability can constrain the student voice on identity. None of the students formulated their version of self primarily through reference to the medical or social model. Instead we found a much more complex notion of identity. As previously identified by Low (1996), Goode (2007) and Olney and Brockelman (2003) it was clear that our students were actively doing work in terms of identity formation: it was not a passive process directed solely by their circumstances.

Nevertheless, there were examples where students used or described the use by others of medical or social model narratives. When students were allocated support based upon their impairments rather than what they considered their individual learning needs this reflected a medical model perspective. Despite the social model's increasing challenge to medical model perspectives within higher education, very few students discussed the social model of disability directly. While a few taking part in this study focused on disabling institutional barriers, others said that they had not experienced discrimination nor did they expect to experience discrimination in the workplace. On the other hand, it was particularly common for teacher trainees (see chapter 7) to feel that they would have to be very careful before disclosing unseen disabilities for fear of workplace discrimination.

Therefore, while there was evidence of medical model and (to a lesser extent) social model narratives operating within and influencing students' accounts of disability, students fully embraced neither model. Instead they can be seen as forming and re-forming their identities within a 'sea' of competing and sometimes conflicting narratives.

Multi-faceted identities

Echoing the findings of Low (1996), Watson (2002) and Goode (2007), disability was not the primary aspect of their identity for students in our study. This is unsurprising given the diversity of participants, who included mature students, mothers, wives, carers, volunteers and employees. Students perceived the core aspects of being a student in different ways. Many students in this project, for example Ben, positioned themselves by reference to a typical student social experience, which for them was closely identified with regularly going to pubs and clubs:

> [We came to] a four-day event where you come and do mock lectures and get handouts on study skills and you go out and get hammered ... Yeah, it was standard, I'd have thought, as any fresher's week would have been, I spent a lot of time in the pub.
>
> (Ben)

Christie *et al.* (2008) note the contrast students entering university from non-traditional backgrounds make between the stereotypical image of student life, with its association with class and privilege, and their own experience of gaining a degree through hard work and dedication. Brandon explicitly described himself as not being a 'waster' which for him was a more important aspect of his identity than social class or disability:

> Probably more of a mentality than a class . . . one of the things at further education college, there was a lot of wasters . . . [but for me] it wasn't the usual student get drunk and party because I just don't do that, it's not me.
>
> (Brandon)

Teresa, a mature student, said she did not want to join in the 'young student' scene. Corinne situated herself outside the mainstream because she had a fiancé who had children.

While some students chose to situate themselves within or outside the social mainstream, students with certain impairments could find themselves excluded because of disabling barriers. For example, one student with epilepsy, Dermot, described being unable to go clubbing with friends because of strobe lighting. Dalia, a wheelchair user, found the sheer number of people at freshers' week social events impossible to negotiate so did not attend them. She also felt she missed out considerably on the social life within her university accommodation as only the ground floor was accessible. Karrie, another wheelchair user, also thought she 'missed out' because she had to go home on the weekends to do her washing and ironing.

Disability and identity – the role of labels

Cara thought 'a lot of people's interpretation of disabled is not being able to walk, being in a wheelchair or being a cripple' and other students also tended to define disability as a permanent, physical and 'extreme' condition, affecting all areas of life:

> I think when I was a kid, I always thought of disabled as either someone who had been very badly maimed, not maimed, but that their limbs wouldn't work, or else someone . . . obviously deaf and stuff like that . . . and Down Syndrome.
>
> (Kathryn)

Disability, in my eyes is more sort of being in a wheelchair or sort of, not being able to speak, something that sort of stops you from doing things on a day to day basis that a normal person would be able to do.

(Dermot)

Students recognised that their own and others' perspectives on 'disability' in the abstract were exaggerated and extremely negative so it is unsurprising that some like Kathryn rejected disability altogether as part of their sense of self:

I don't like it, I have to say, it's not something that I feel very comfortable with. I have never classified myself as disabled. If I was going to label it would be diabetic.

(Kathryn)

Anne felt similarly:

Oh, god there is such a stigma. If I ever said to someone 'I am disabled' they would think 'well you're not in a wheelchair, what's going on?' Also a learning difficulty, I don't like that either cause it kind of sounds like I need a minder or something . . . So I don't describe myself as disabled.

(Anne)

Deal (2002) has argued that there is a 'hierarchy of impairments' amongst disabled people whereby disabled people do not always wish to be associated with other impairment groups, for a variety of reasons. Holland *et al.* (1998) describe how borderline categories (in their case, categories of mental illness) can allow individuals a certain latitude in how they respond to their disabled status in different contexts. So, for example, dyslexic students tended to argue that although they had dyslexia, they were either not disabled or only 'borderline':

I think disabled implies a physical disability rather than mental. And I guess in some ways dyslexia is a disability but I don't think it is necessarily an appropriate term for it. Partly because . . . it is not most people's idea of [disability].

(James)

I don't particularly mind it [being labelled 'disabled'] but I don't sort of think it's really appropriate for, kind of, for dyslexics, personally, because they're not exactly that disabled, you know.

(Darren)

Riddell notes that 'high numbers of students in certain categories, for example dyslexia, indicate that this is an area where declaring a disability is likely to provide access to resources (word processing equipment, extra time in exams) without incurring a negative label' (1998: 211). This relative lack of stigma is likely to be due to dyslexia's status as a hidden or borderline disability and its distance from students' negative conceptions of 'disability', which tended to be associated with physical impairments. This would also help to explain why several students opted to disclose only dyslexia when they had more than one impairment (see below).

For some the label of disabled student was situational or context-specific – they might take on the label because it facilitated access to reasonable adjustments, but did not consider themselves to be disabled, or only in the context of learning support, as Low (1996) and Olney and Brockelman (2003) also document. Disability was only part of Duncan's identity in the university setting:

I do describe myself as a disabled student, when my mates and stuff ask, it's like, how did you get this and how do you get the extra time and stuff, that's how I describe myself, but that's not how I describe myself out of university.

(Duncan)

Daisy and Billy had a similar perspective:

It does give you access to all sorts of things because if you don't say 'I'm disabled' you don't get the support. You have to understand that you need the support in order to get where you want to be. Otherwise, if you don't have any support then you would find it impossible to do anything, like uni[versity]-wise.

(Daisy)

I didn't really see myself as kind of disabled until I went for help with this because I'd seen you can get help with disabled stuff. And I thought, oh right, I can utilise this. Until that point I didn't categorise myself as anything.

(Billy)

Overall, students with a variety of impairments were likely to feel more positive about the label of 'disabled students' when it was linked to support. Other students accepted that disability was, as Andrew said: 'part of me, it is not my defining characteristic'.

> I wouldn't like to think of it as my main identity . . . But, if people see me as 'that chap's got epilepsy' then that's the way they see it but hopefully, it isn't a big glowing sort of thing that says I've got epilepsy just beware. I prefer to be thought of as a normal person.
>
> (Dermot)

Feeling 'different' and being 'normal'

For both the medical and social models of disability, to be 'disabled' is to be 'different' from non-disabled people, whether this difference is caused by the limitations of the individual or society's imposition of barriers. When some students talked about feeling 'different' in relation to disability this was as the opposite of 'normal'. Cara's account was typical:

> And I think if you're a 'normal' student, you can adapt to that sort of, but for a pupil with disabilities, dyslexia or depression or both in my case . . . it's kind of like, . . . putting a fish in deep water, you kind of do feel a bit out of your depth.
>
> (Cara)

However, some students were working towards a different understanding of difference, as variation within normal limits – something that might perhaps be better captured by the broader concept of 'diversity', as a positive aspect of their identity to be valued rather than minimised or normalised. Bella's lecturer (Lecturer Brand), adopting an affirmative model of disability (Swain and French, 2000), referred to the idea of dyslexia being a good kind of difference:

> All our artistic programmes have a very high level of dyslexic students because of again what we do. In my understanding there is a clear relationship between dyslexia and levels of creativity.
>
> (Lecturer Brand)

However, generally students were keen not to feel different. Instead, while several students accepted or adopted the 'disabled' label, they simultaneously saw themselves as 'normal'. These students can be seen as potentially challenging the idea that disability necessarily implies 'difference'.

Some were able to reconcile these apparently contradictory states by seeing themselves as normal with limitations. Jean said: 'We all have strands and areas of development that can be worked on' which Andrew agreed with: 'We have all got things we can and can't do'.

Some students were clearly more comfortable thinking about their impairment as just one way in which they were different from their friends. Ben explained how he was teased for his poor spelling, but that all other group members could expect to be teased:

> There's like 20 of us in our group, and we're all . . . banter gets passed round, So it's something that I have, that I am, so it's something that gets mentioned. But equally then, other people get stick for different things, so it's nothing that I find offensive or inappropriate.
>
> (Ben)

Several students seemed to define being 'normal' to fit in with being disabled. For example, Andrew thought that 'in a sense there is a very fine line between being disabled and being, for want of a better word, "normal" if you know what I mean'. For others the concepts were not incompatible:

> When I'm ill, yeah, I would say I'm classed as disabled but times like this, I think well I'm just, like the next person. I think it's quite good actually, to see, that you can be classed as disabled, but still lead a perfectly, sort of, normal life.
>
> (Dionne)

Dermot and Dionne both had unpredictable illnesses and dealt with the implications of disability for their own identity in different ways. Dermot describes disability as something permanent and so argues that he does not have a disability, while Dionne says that she is disabled when she is ill, but not at other times.

Being independent

For many students, university represents a move towards independence and for the disabled students in our project this interacted in different ways with the issue of receiving support. Receiving visible learning support was a key signifier of difference to staff and other students. A common view was that it was not 'normal' to ask for or receive support additional to that of the 'normal' student, meaning that achieving 'independence' – not receiving the officially allocated assistance – was particularly important for some students. Ben's conception of independence was typical:

> I've always been quite independent, so I've never really asked for anything unless I've really needed it. And with everything last year [Year 1] I didn't feel that I needed any support with anything, so I never really asked.
>
> (Ben)

Not asking for help was a matter of pride for Andrew which was also linked to a reluctance to disclose an impairment if it meant being treated 'differently':

> My mum doesn't understand, she doesn't understand why I don't ask for help but it's just being totally proud . . . I don't want people to treat me any differently so I don't tend to mention it to anyone, not even the lecturers.
>
> (Andrew)

Alan stated that the most important learning for him at university was learning to live independently. Kathryn talked about the importance of being able to look after herself, especially in the context of managing her diabetes. Interestingly, Billy saw independence as asking other people for help (in preference to receiving unsolicited help), but this was not a common view.

Emotional work and discursive labour

Reeve (2002) highlights the psycho-emotional effects of disability, while Goode (2007) describes the emotional implications of being a disabled student at university. The dilemmas and emotional 'work' that accompany the negotiation of a disabled student identity were patent in our project. Students described a range of coping strategies for their learning that had the potential to be emotionally exhausting – of always having to be practical, to plan ahead, to stay alert and think of contingencies. Students with unpredictable illnesses such as epilepsy or depression were particularly likely to be concerned about the consequences of not feeling in control. Daisy, Cara and Jean all talked about having to 'fight'. Dalia and Karrie, both wheelchair users, used humour (one of Low's tactics of negotiation) as a coping strategy to deal with events that could otherwise be viewed as very traumatic. Other students talked about being strong-willed or having a positive outlook as a coping strategy. For Alan, it was a question of just 'getting on with things', not wanting to claim sympathy for his impairments as he saw himself as responsible for his learning. Jean was unwilling to request reasonable adjustments for fear of stigma and came up with several alternative coping strategies of her own.

All the participants in the project would have had to talk about their impairments with someone at university, if only in the process of accessing disabled status on arrival. However, some took on a much greater burden of explanation when the impairment in question was in some way borderline, either because the individual did not see themselves as disabled but chose to access support, or because the disabled status of the condition is itself sometimes disputed in the public domain, as is the case with dyslexia. Holland *et al.* (1998) noted the 'inordinate amount of discursive labour' which one of their participants with borderline personality disorder devoted to working on his identity, and there was evidence that some of our project participants were similarly working through different narratives about disability to find a position with which they felt comfortable. Barry, who had declared dyslexia, called on medical and social narratives to account for his particular pattern of difficulties:

> I developed my tinnitus at the age of ten . . . but also I have nystagmus problems with my eyes as well . . . I wear glasses for reading but it's the brain signal and the ear and everything like that you know . . . it was the seventies then and basically . . . they took us out of the class, put us on tables outside in the corridor – all glass doors so all the kids could see that we were separate from them . . . It was totally wrong, which obviously I know now – but we were just shoved in the corridor really because at that time they called it remedial education, so we got the label of 'Rem' really which stuck with me for many, many years – that has more of a detrimental effect on you than the lack of the education because it's such a big handle to take through school.
>
> (Barry)

The dilemmas of disclosure

Dilemmas over disclosure exist for many students (see also chapters 3, 5 and 7), particularly those with an unseen disability. Whether or not to disclose is problematic because disclosure may mean being treated differently by staff and other students. There was a 'trade off' between the potential adverse effects of stigma associated with disclosure and the necessity of accessing support for their learning. Many students actively stated their wish to be treated the same as other students and not to be treated differently. This was particularly the case for students who had not previously accessed support in an educational environment.

Nonetheless, several of the students taking part in this project (mostly those with visible impairments or dyslexia – especially if they had struggled to be recognised as dyslexic in school) were unconcerned about disclosing their impairment, seeing it as a straightforward means of accessing support. 'I've lived with it so long; you don't hide it any more' (Dionne). When asked if he had any concerns about disclosure, Ben replied:

> No, not really. It was more the fact that I knew there would be help available if I did, so I thought I might as well.
>
> (Ben)

Cara had disclosed dyslexia to the university but not depression, because of her fear of stigma, both for mental health problems and for having two diagnoses. Her position supports Deal's (2002) hierarchy of impairments, already discussed:

> It sounds bad to have two disabilities rather than just one . . . I'd probably say I had a disability as my dyslexia rather than my depression because if you say dyslexia, one, people don't know what it is and don't understand the ins and outs of it and secondly it doesn't have a big stigma like depression. You say depression and it's like 'oooh'.
>
> (Cara)

Cara saw her dyslexia diagnosis positively as it enabled her to obtain support and, interestingly, she also found that many of the support strategies provided for dyslexia (e.g. PC, extra time in exams) also helped her to manage her depression, both so that it did not affect her learning and so her learning activities did not adversely affect her mental health.

There is some evidence, however, that the range of categories of disability recognised by the university might constrain students' decisions about what information to pass on. Barry disclosed dyslexia, yet his medical problems, which were still undiagnosed when he started his course, impacted more seriously on his progress on his chosen course than dyslexia. Choosing to be categorised as dyslexic was, however, a positive move for Barry because it helped him to make sense of his difficulties in school, whereas choosing to be classified as medically unfit must have been less appealing since his medical problems had just cost him his job. Similarly, Billy's declaration of mobility impairment masked the much greater struggle he had with taking on a university course as a recovering drug addict; the latter, however, was not available as a category for support. These examples show how the rigidity of the universities' systems of support-tied-to-disclosure meant that students had to position themselves in particular ways to receive support, which might not reflect how they really saw themselves.

Several students contacted the Disability Office late because they thought they could cope or did not want to make a fuss. Asking for help could be triggered by a crisis or more often by being informed about support available or being encouraged by student peers. The involvement of student peers might have helped disabled students to see obtaining support as more 'normal'. Alternatively, this late accessing of support could be seen as part of a process of becoming more comfortable with their impairments in the context of university or more generally, as their identities altered. Some students appeared to become more accepting and relaxed about the disability label and disclosure as their university careers developed. For example, James's attitude changed from not seeing himself as requiring much support to recognising that specific support could be useful. Billy noticed a change in his attitude between years 1 and 2, from 'can't do that', to 'yes you can, but take your time'.

The stigma of the disability label and lack of information, whether for students about available support (see chapter 3) or for staff about appropriate reasonable adjustments (see chapter 5) meant that some students did not disclose their disability, with adverse effects for their learning. This raises questions over the extent to which university support systems rely on disabled students being proactive about accessing support if they fall through 'cracks' in the system or if disability only became apparent later in the course. This suggests that students with less forceful personalities might miss out on support, at least initially.

Summary

Students' accounts clearly demonstrate the complexity and contextual nature of identity formation and negotiation for disabled students within higher education. Given the negativity of the dominant societal narrative on disability, the medical model, it is perhaps understandable that disability was not a key aspect of identity for the disabled students in our study. Students used a range of sophisticated strategies to minimise or separate themselves from the 'disabled' label as part of their sense of self. However, the social model of disability was similarly unhelpful for exploring the lived experience of identity, because it, too, is predicated upon societal construction of disability as 'difference' from the norm, rather than as part of the range of human variation.

It was clear from their use of terminology that it was very important for students to perceive themselves, and to believe that others perceived them, as 'normal' (which helps to explain why disability was often not viewed as a core aspect of identity). However, the categories and structures used to define and manage disability within higher education can actively hinder students' desires to see themselves (and be seen by others) as a 'normal' student. Disclosing an impairment or visibly receiving learning support actively marked some students out as 'different' from their peers, and the emotional effects of this experience were clear. The perceived stigma of disclosure often meant that reasonable adjustments were not requested or put in place.

The responses of other students trying to negotiate an atypical student identity in the study by Christie *et al.* (2008) of students from non-traditional backgrounds raise the possibility that 'normal' is becoming a contested issue for students in UK institutions:

> In many instances there is a conscious rejection of the assumed norms of a middle-class student life and a clear sense that [widening access students] should have a right to establish a different way of being a student in the 21st century.
>
> (Christie *et al.*, 2005: 26)

Being disabled is another way of being judged and found to be different alongside the differences in class and financial security which

Christie's respondents highlighted, and adds to the emotional work entailed in negotiating a student identity within higher education. Given the degree of emotional work involved, it was rational for some students to seek to project a non-disabled identity, as previous studies have found (Low, 1996; Goode, 2007). However, from our analysis, it appears that other disabled students are re-defining narratives of disability so that the experience of disability is made compatible with being 'normal'. Some of these students argued that disability was just one type of variation within normal limits, while others questioned the 'fine line' between disability and normality. This was a process that appeared to develop over time, in tandem for some with becoming more positive about their identity as a disabled student.

The affirmation model of disability emphasises the positive social identity of disability and Swain and French (2003: 160) argue that 'in affirming a positive identity of being impaired, disabled people are actively repudiating the dominant nature of normality'. They criticise the social model for merely re-defining the 'problem' of disability, arguing that their model considers more accurately the implications for identity of opposition to the disability-as-personal-tragedy perspective. However, they also consider the reasons why some disabled people might not adopt the affirmation model for themselves; for example, if an impairment is newly acquired the person will be steeped in the 'dominant social values' of the personal tragedy model (Swain and French, 2003: 154). Some students in our study (e.g. Jean) continued to attach negative connotations to their impairment label throughout their course, although attitudes did appear to become more relaxed over time.

The continuing dominance of the personal tragedy/medical model perspective through institutional systems, categories and the attitudes of staff, peers and the students themselves has implications for the way support is offered and delivered. For as long as 'reasonable adjustments' remain as standardised sets of procedures enacted for a legitimised few, they will continue to stigmatise those they seek to benefit, in particular by marking them out as 'different'. Chapter 4 argues that a move from assimilative (or individual) reasonable adjustments towards inclusive adjustments (for all learners) will benefit the learning experience of all students. This chapter supports these conclusions by demonstrating that students' conceptions of their impairment are not aligned to rigid institutional categories, and that disabled students actively seek to reject separateness or difference as part of their identity, which can have negative implications for their learning. Any move, therefore, towards a more universal expectation that all students might access reasonable adjustments in the form of advice, strategies and support with learning, will lessen the effects of the 'disabled' label, as the concept of 'learning support' becomes mainstream.

Chapter 7

The idea of fitness to practise

Discourses of disability and the negotiation of identity in initial teacher training

Sheila Riddell and Elisabet Weedon

Introduction

In this chapter, we use case studies of disabled students taking Initial Teacher Training (ITT) courses at University 1, a Scottish pre-1992 university, to explore the way in which their identity as disabled students is handled in different contexts and articulates with wider aspects of identity formation. For most students, there is a separation between life as a student and life as a worker, and it may be possible to include disability as part of one's identity at university, while subsequently abandoning it on moving into the workplace. For students with impairments which are visible to others, disability is likely to be a constant aspect of their identity, but for the majority who have unseen impairments, there may be a degree of choice as to whether disability is a permanent or transient feature of identity.

Students in vocational areas of study such as Education, who undertake teaching placements alongside their academic studies, are a particularly interesting group to study, since the process of professional enculturation runs in parallel to other aspects of identity formation. In addition, the idea of 'fitness to practise' (which draws on a particular discourse of disability, the medical model), requires students to position themselves in relation to a disabled identity in the workplace and to make decisions about disclosure at the workplace.

In this chapter, the following questions are addressed, particularly drawing on case studies of two ITT students at University 1, Jean and Andrew:

- How is 'fitness to practise' understood formally and informally in relation to ITT?

- Do ideas about 'fitness to teach' appear to have had an impact on the student's decision to disclose an impairment?
- At what point, if at all, do ITT students choose to disclose an impairment at university and on teaching placement, and why?
- What has been the effect of disclosure on the individual's access to resources, reasonable adjustments and identity in the university and on teaching placement?
- How do ITT students understand their impairment and how does this understanding appear to have evolved during the course of their school experience, university education and transition to the workplace?

Fitness to practise standards in teaching

Disabled people's entry to the professions has traditionally been restricted by the assumption that they might pose a risk to the general public, reflected in fitness to practise standards. For example, the Nursing and Midwifery Council, which regulates the nursing profession in England, Wales and Scotland, maintains that nurses must be of 'good health and good character' and operates fitness testing at the point of registration. Entry to teaching, medicine and social work are similarly controlled by regulatory bodies, although the standards are framed differently in the various professional arenas and applied differently in different jurisdictions of the UK.

The General Teaching Council for Scotland was established in 1965 to regulate the teaching profession and fitness to practise standards were formalised in regulations introduced in 1993. Applicants for teacher training had to satisfy the medical practitioner for the particular institution that they were 'medically fit to teach'. Teaching in Scotland differs from the other caring professions in that, following a consultation in 2004 (Scottish Executive, 2004), it was decided to remove the fitness to practise standards on the grounds that they were anachronistic and ineffective in identifying individuals who might pose a risk to children. The document notes that the medical standards were initially introduced to protect children from infectious diseases such as tuberculosis, but such conditions are now quite rare and would only be detected in the later stages. Conditions such as HIV would only be detectable if laboratory tests were carried out, which were not part of the medical examination, and individuals with blood born viruses might well be asymptomatic. Psychiatric problems, it was noted, might also pose a threat to children, but there was no degree of

certainty in relation to identifying which candidates might be danger-
ous. The General Teaching Council for Scotland published a General
Code of Practice and competency standards for full registration (GTCS,
2002) which were deemed to supersede the requirement for separate
health and fitness checks, particularly in light of the extension of
the Disability Discrimination Act (DDA) to cover the activities of professional regulatory bodies. Despite the abolition of the fitness to
practise standards, employers of teachers in Scotland require future
employees to disclose whether they are disabled and, if deemed necessary by an occupational health practitioner, to undergo a medical
examination.

By way of contrast to the situation in Scotland, the Department for
Education and Skills in England still insists that entrants to ITT and
qualified teachers meet standards on physical and mental fitness to
teach. These standards are set out in Circular 4/99 (DfEE, 1999)
which explains the Secretary of State's powers to 'bar' a teacher on
'medical grounds' under 1993 Regulations, which have since been
repealed. The Circular appears to contain two possibly contradictory
messages, one suggesting that teaching may be an unsuitable career
for disabled people, the other pointing to the benefits of including a
higher proportion of disabled people in the teaching workforce. It
states:

> Teachers and those training to become teachers need a high
> standard of physical and mental health to enter or remain in the
> teaching profession as teaching is a demanding career and teachers
> have to act in loco parentis for the pupils in their charge. The
> health, education, safety and welfare of pupils are important in
> deciding on an individual's fitness to teach.
>
> (DfEE, 1999: B1.1)

Shortly afterwards, a slightly different message is given:

> Disabled staff can make an important contribution to the overall
> school curriculum, both as effective employees and in raising the
> aspirations of disabled pupils and educating non-disabled people
> about the reality of disability. Many disabled people will be med-
> ically fit to teach, though employers may have to make reasonable
> adjustments under the DDA to enable disabled people to carry out
> their duties effectively.
>
> (DfEE, 1999: B2.1)

The Pensions and Medical Fitness School Workforce Group of the Department for Education and Skills drafted amendments to the Circular to make it compliant with the DDA.

The Disability Rights Commission undertook a formal general investigation into Fitness to Practise standards in teaching, nursing and social work (DRC, 2007) and concluded that these discriminated against disabled people in these professions, leading them to conceal their impairments or to leave their chosen profession early, reflected by the very low numbers of disabled people in these fields. The DRC also argued that the standards acted as a deterrent to disabled people who were considering entry to the profession, and that occupational health tests applied by prospective employers might also deter disabled people from applying for teaching jobs, rather than being used to identify the reasonable adjustments which might be helpful, as required by the DDA.

This perception is confirmed by data submitted by the General Teaching Council for Scotland (GTCS) (2007), which shows that, while disabled students make up about 3 per cent of all disabled students in Education, they account for a much smaller proportion of teachers on the Teacher Induction Scheme (the one year school-based programme which all Education graduates undertake after their initial training). The number and percentage of teachers on the induction scheme is shown in Table 7.1.

The case studies which we present later are of two students who entered an ITT course at a time when the fitness standards were still operational, although these were abolished during the course of their four-year period of study. One student had an unseen impairment (dyslexia) and the other had cerebral palsy which affected his mobility, but which often allowed him to pass as non-disabled. Studying the

Table 7.1 Number and percentage of disabled and non-disabled teachers on the Teacher Induction Scheme in Scotland, 2002–2006

Year	Disabled teachers	Non-disabled teachers
2002	12 (0.59%)	2,009 (99.4%)
2003	6 (0.3%)	1,808 (99.7%)
2004	16 (1.2%)	2,018 (98.8%)
2005	24 (0.89%)	2,670 (99.1%)
2006	31 (1.1%)	3,509 (98.9%)

Source: GTCS submission to DRC in 2007

experiences of those with unseen, or almost unseen, impairments is particularly important, since they represent by far the largest group of disabled students, and, precisely because of the invisibility of their condition, face dilemmas in relation to disclosure at many points in their personal and professional lives. The case studies illustrate the individual's profound ambivalence in relation to the category of disability, and the way in which the external environment either encourages or precludes disclosure (see also chapter 6). In addition they illustrate the high degree of anxiety provoked by pressure to prove that one is fit to practise as a teacher, even though the requirement for a formal medical examination was abandoned in 2004.

Case study one: Jean

Jean was a married mature student with three children who had decided to return to higher education to study a course which would allow her to find local employment. Her husband, a fire fighter, worked shifts and was therefore available to help out with childcare. She was from a working-class background and her siblings had taken very different life courses:

> My dad was a woodcutter and saw miller and my mum was a stay-at-home mum, my sister worked in a shop – she is now a beauty therapist, she has been to college [and has got an HND] . . . my other brother, he is doing fantastically . . . he is the top company manager for Asia . . . he speaks fluent Japanese, he is married to a Japanese woman, but he started working from the bottom up . . . My other brother is a JCB digger and does motor cross racing.
>
> (Jean)

Jean experienced literacy difficulties at school, but dyslexia was eventually identified when she went for her medical prior to beginning teacher training. Jean was among the last required to undergo the examination and in the course of a discussion about her general health she disclosed worries about her spelling. Rather than using this as a reason for barring Jean from entry to teacher training, the doctor suggested that she might have a dyslexic-type difficulty which could be managed with reasonable adjustments on the course and in the workplace. Indeed, the doctor herself experienced similar difficulties:

> Then in my medical she asked me 'Do you have [spelling prob-
> lems]?' because I was so petrified with my application form that I
> had spelt something wrong, so I had everybody checking it and
> I was like 'I do . . . but will that hold me back from getting in?'
> and she said 'No, it shouldn't at all'. And she was a doctor and it
> had never held her back.
>
> (Jean)

Following appointments with the disability adviser and an educational
psychologist, dyslexia was formally diagnosed and the Disabled Students Allowance awarded. However, the process was lengthy and support in the form of a laptop and software packages was not available
until the second year of the course.

Disability and identity

Jean felt that there was a real stigma attached to having reading and
writing difficulties:

> I come from a generation where it was looked on very badly
> and you were regarded as being stupid and dunce and things like
> that . . . I didn't tell my mum for ages.
>
> (Jean)

As a result, she was wary of discussing her diagnosis of dyslexia even
with close family and friends and had an ambivalent relationship with
the concept of disability:

> I don't like the word . . . not able, because of the 'dis'. I don't like it
> and I still don't know . . . I still won't class myself as disabled.
>
> (Jean)

She went on to explain her image of a disabled person as a wheelchair
user, even though she saw this as 'shocking' and 'awful' in revealing
her own prejudices. As for most of the disabled students in this study,
being categorised as a disabled student did not sit easily with her
overall sense of self (see chapter 6):

> I still get emails from the Disability Office to register with [a
> disability group]. I kind of think 'I am not disabled' . . . I mean
> there is one argument that, you know, labelling it might give you

more resources and yeah, it has given me extra time which I am
really pleased with . . . but then I kind of think well, I don't know.

(Jean)

Experiences of teaching, learning and assessment

Jean's course involved a mixture of academic work in the university
and placements in school. In the university, the Director of Studies was
intended to inform all tutors about her requirements for reasonable
adjustments, but this happened in a somewhat haphazard manner.
Some lecturers were very sympathetic, adapting their teaching style
and providing emotional support:

And at the end of the workshop I was just upset [about the difficulties posed by dyslexia] . . . and I spoke to her and was saying
'What can I do [about my dyslexia?]'. She was like 'See this as a
positive thing, this is going to make you a better teacher for the
children who have struggled, that you will be able to identify with
their struggles'.

(Jean)

Other lecturers had a rather more casual teaching style and did not
appear to make any allowances for the difficulties experienced by
some students:

When the overheads are up I make a point of always sitting at
the front so I can see what is going and you know you can hear
the lecturer and I am not distracted by people chatting about
what they have done at the weekend or texting or whatever . . .
She [the lecturer] actually moved more into the group so visually
I am not seeing her because she is obviously aware that there
are people chatting about what they've done at the weekend . . .
so she is trying to catch their attention. So she moves into the
group as overheads are swishing on and off, she is talking about
something else which is so important that I am supposed to be
taking [it] down and I am a bit like . . . 'What do you want me
to do?'

(Jean)

Lecturers within the School of Education had radically different
understanding of and sympathy towards the needs of students with a

diagnosis of dyslexia and the suitability of teaching as a career for disabled people more generally:

> There is a feeling amongst teacher trainers that there is a bottom line in terms of showing the children correct grammar, correct spelling, correct English, whatever. And if you are going to teach and you are writing worksheets for children where the grammar is wrong or the spelling is wrong or your notes on the board are full of errors, then somehow you are giving less than decent education to youngsters . . . On the other hand, I am big enough to realise that some spelling errors on the board may be completely over-balanced by a cracking good personality and planning and engaging with the children.
>
> (Lecturer Archer)

Others felt that the university lecturers themselves were sometimes deficient in their knowledge of disability issues and the values which they were modelling for their students:

> There are people teaching on the social justice and inclusion course who have no awareness of some of the issues around or preferences of people with particular disabilities.
>
> (Lecturer Avery)

Despite the variability of practical and emotional support, Jean felt that her university experience had been largely positive and the adjustments made, in terms of extra time in exams and access to lecture notes in advance, were adequate. However, as illustrated later, her experience of school placement was much more difficult.

Teaching placement

Jean had one main placement during second year, a five-week period in a nursery, when she decided not to disclose her dyslexia because the placement was very short. However, she devised a notetaking system in order to retain information about pupils and parents. Aspects of staff room culture caused her concern on this teaching placement:

> They would make a comment about when a parent had come in and said 'I am concerned my child may be dyslexic'. There was a little girl who was showing signs of dyspraxia, always walking on

her tiptoes, and there were a few comments, not from the head teacher, not from the teacher but from the other staff. And it might not have been the main staff, it might even have been the auxiliary, classroom assistant . . . I felt a little bit like it was unprofessional and one part of me did feel like saying something . . . but I didn't in the end.

(Jean)

In Year 3, the students were on placement for almost the whole of semester one and issues arose around disclosure. This created considerable problems for Jean and left her feeling unhappy about her relationship with the first teacher on her teaching practice. She was also upset about the manner in which she was challenged by her Director of Studies (DoS) in relation to disclosure and whether she really ought to be a teacher:

I spoke to her [DoS] and she was a bit like, 'Well you are going to have to explain to the school as it is, because when you do your probationer year it has to be disclosed'. So I was really shocked by that and felt very bruised that this was going to have to happen, and then she actually questioned whether I should be teaching in the first place.

(Jean)

Jean decided to discuss her dyslexia with her first placement teacher after having proved she was sufficiently competent:

I told my teacher at the end of my first week, beginning of my second, because I had got some major things done and I thought 'Well, she knows that I am a hard worker . . .' and her expression was, I will never forget, her expression was 'Really!' And I just said to her 'Yes, you know I cope' and stuff and then the next day I went in and she was very close to another teacher in the school, and I felt like I had been discussed, and there was kind of looks being made and things, and then that teacher, from then onwards treated me like a child, and was very, very picky.

(Jean)

The teacher had some problems in compiling a report and so the head teacher was asked to confirm that Jean's performance was adequate. As a result, Jean decided against future disclosure:

So that was hard, I cried a lot in those three weeks, and I was worried about going back to the same school, that it was going to have a knock on effect . . . I didn't think the head knew and I did wonder about speaking to the head but there was a lot of animosity between the head and the teachers . . . I felt like [the] primary one teacher and definitely the primary four/five teacher who are very close had discussed it.

(Jean)

She was awarded straight As for this placement by the university assessor and felt vindicated. However, the experience taught her that there were considerable dangers in disclosing an impairment, since this seemed to result in suspicion which was likely to undermine confidence.

Jean also discussed the practical difficulties she encountered, mainly in the area of spelling, and her coping strategies:

Yes, I made mistakes spelling . . . one of the wee girls said 'Mrs M you have spelt that wrong' and I said 'oh, really.' I still struggle with el/le endings . . . What I used to do was I sometimes have prompt cards and I would kind of pre-empt what would come up . . . I mean when I go round and kids would say . . . 'how do you write . . .?' I would say 'let's have a look . . . tell you what, you go and check the dictionary'. So I tend to do those strategies. If I had my own class I would probably say 'Oh, you know I am not very good at spelling but it doesn't mean we shouldn't keep trying'.

(Jean)

Jean's experiences of life as a trainee teacher were thus extremely mixed, and, although she completed the course successfully, the dangers of disclosure were clearly underlined. We now turn to a second case study, Andrew, an Education student with a diagnosis of cerebral palsy.

Case study two: Andrew

Andrew was in his twenties and had attended a state comprehensive school in a relatively disadvantaged area before undertaking an HND at a further education college. Subsequently he was admitted to a university at some distance from his home to undertake ITT in primary education. He was the first member of his family to participate in higher education. Andrew lived at home, resulting in a long cross-country bus journey to and from the university. Part of the reason for this was to enable him to support his disabled mother.

Andrew was a premature baby and as a result experienced some impairment of motor function which affected his mobility and co-ordination. His impairment was not immediately obvious, and he often chose to 'pass' as a non-disabled person. Despite having a close group of friends, Andrew did not mention his impairment until well into his second year:

> I happened to mention that I was three months premature blah, blah, blah and my friend [name] said 'has that left you with any-thing?' she was just asking. And I said, 'Well, it has actually' and I just explained to her and she said 'You'd never know that, you don't really notice it'. Which is good.
>
> (Andrew)

At college, he received excellent support from the student disability advisor, who helped him claim Disabled Students Allowance. His experience at university, however, was far more variable. His first meeting with a disability advisor led to him being told that his impair-ment was not severe enough to warrant additional support, despite the fact that his medical records had been sent on from the college. In second year, however, he met a different disability advisor who quickly arranged for him to have additional IT support.

Disability and identity

While recognising that he had an impairment, Andrew was reluctant to make this the defining feature of his identity. He did not feel he had been discriminated against, did not see himself as disabled and rejected the idea of being treated differently because of his impair-ment. In an interview in third year he commented:

> I have never let it bother me, it's funny. I know that I am impaired to a certain extent and I am lucky that my impairment isn't a lot more severe. To me it just means that you might take longer to do things . . . but at the end of the day it doesn't stop you doing things . . . You just need to learn to adapt . . . I have never really thought

'I can't do this and I can't do that'. I just think 'I can do that and if I run into trouble I will cross that bridge when I come to it'.

(Andrew)

However, he recognised that there were certain things which were difficult or impossible:

Definitely [difficult] – a lot of things. PE and things ... but again you just kind of say 'well I can do it to a certain extent' so I know my limits. You do it to your limit and stop and say 'I can't do any more'.

(Andrew)

As a result of his desire to be treated the same as others, Andrew discussed his impairment with very few people:

So if you were to approach any of the lecturers ... they wouldn't know because I don't tell them. I mean my circle of friends knows and they have seen it ... My legs are particularly bad at night time. When I am tired I start to fall over myself ... I don't tell anyone because it's the whole pride thing, it is because I don't want anyone to treat me differently.

(Andrew)

Part of the reason for saying little about his impairment was to avoid criticism or resentment from other students:

I don't want people to say 'Oh, look at him, he's getting extra time' because I do see it. People in the course look at another girl who is disabled and they say 'Oh, look at her, she's got a laptop'. I don't want that. I don't want to be ostracised like that, so that's why I don't mention it.

(Andrew)

Andrew recognised that there were times when he needed to disclose, for example, to negotiate an alternative assignment on an Environmental Studies field trip:

The river study was one particular thing ... They accommodated me really well. They just said 'you don't need to do that' but one of the assistants took me in the van and we went to a visitor centre and I evaluated the usefulness of the visitor centre. I was doing something, although it was different to the rest of them, I wasn't just sitting in the cabin with my feet up.

(Andrew)

Even receiving extra time in exams caused Andrew some degree of social embarrassment:

It is not something that I really like doing. I explained it to those who really needed to know and as for the rest of them well – I just left them guessing. All they knew was that I was up at [place name]. They didn't know the reason. That was fine. I just said I had a wee bit extra time just to read over it more carefully. That was fine.

(Andrew)

Experiences of teaching, learning and assessment

The only adjustments which Andrew received during his time at university were assistance with IT equipment, extra time in exams and some flexibility over deadlines. As was the case with Jean, his lecturers demonstrated very different understandings of disability.

All three lecturers thought that there were specific issues in relation to disabled students doing teacher training. However, they differed in terms of the extent to which they felt that disabled students could become 'fit to practise' and in the way that they tackled making reasonable adjustments. Lecturer Adams, for example, whilst being willing to make some adjustments, felt that some students were simply 'too disabled' to teach:

In general I don't think we can make broad changes to the curriculum. The teaching courses are slightly different from the average academic course in that these people are all trained to be teachers. They can't be too disabled or the question would arise about what they are going to do in the classroom . . . We [the department] have never met together and said 'in general [how do we respond] . . . what we do is to respond to needs that we are informed about'.

(Lecturer Adams)

Lecturer Anderson considered that the institution had not managed to increase awareness of disability amongst staff as a result of competing priorities:

> I actually don't ever speak about these issues with my colleagues on a day to day basis . . . If the institution had done a good job of raising our awareness, it may well be putting things on our agenda to talk about on a regular basis . . . On our agendas are bums on seats, recruitments, financial income, new building plans – those sort of things occupy our time.
>
> (Lecturer Anderson)

The lack of awareness and informed debate about disability issues was also strongly emphasised by Lecturer Armstrong, who was a recent recruit with a background in special needs education:

> I am inclined to say 'DDA what DDA?' People just don't seem to know about it . . . I am constantly taken aback by the sorts of discussion that are had that I would have imagined taking place five years ago.
>
> (Lecturer Armstrong)

Lecturers felt that the GTCS needed greater clarity about the concept of fitness to practise and its operationalisation:

> The whole question of who actually decides whether this disabled person is fit to come on the course is not clear. The GTC won't give you a straight answer, or they didn't to me.
>
> (Lecturer Adams)

An alternative view was presented by Lecturer Armstrong, who felt that students could benefit greatly from being taught by someone who themselves experienced difficulties.

Teaching placement

While placements in Years 1 and 2 were relatively successful, Andrew experienced major problems in relation to his placement in year three, although these were triggered by his mother's illness rather than his impairment. He found the school unsympathetic, thus heightening his anxiety, and in the end decided to take some time out and redo the placement:

By the Friday I was completely scunnered. I don't mind construc-
tive criticism but it had got to the point where I felt they were
knifing me in the back every time he [teacher] said there was
something wrong with my lesson, it was just like pure knife in my
back . . . My mum would phone me at lunch time and I would end
up crying to her on the phone. That's not me, I am not that emotional . . . I got home on the Friday and I phoned the school and
said 'I am making an appointment with the doctor' . . . I said 'it is
nothing to do with the school . . . it's just me – I need to get myself
sorted out . . .' She seemed fine and then she kind of put the boot
in a bit and said 'Clearly that is your decision but I would advise
you to work through it' . . . I said to her 'I am sorry my lessons
haven't been up to scratch . . . it is just because I am going through
some things' . . . Then she really dug in and said 'Well, yes, from
what I have seen you don't have what it takes to be a primary
teacher'. I thought, 'Yes, kick me in the ribs when I am down'.

(Andrew)

Finally, the placement was completed over the summer in his old primary school, which meant he was less tired and much less stressed. On
the basis of this experience, Andrew decided that he would disclose his
impairment to a future employer in order to ensure that reasonable
adjustments could be made, particularly with regard to flexible deadlines to avoid over-tiredness and anxiety.

Discussion

We began this chapter by discussing the contradictory imperatives in
late capitalist societies in relation to disability. On the one hand, as
observed by Stone (1984), disability clearly serves as a category of
administrative convenience, justifying the exclusion of a large section
of the population from the labour market who are often disadvantaged
by poverty and exclusion rather than by impairment. Running alongside this discourse are at least two others. The idea of disability as
stigma, as described by Goffman (1990), still persists, leading people
to interpret impairments as a shameful marker of physical or mental
imperfection and consequently making disability an unattractive identity for many people to accept. Counteracting this are the efforts of the
disability movement and the Disability Rights Commission, which
have sought to establish disability as a political category by promoting
positive images of disabled people, drawing on discourses of difference

rather than deficit. Clearly, these competing discourses around disability have knock-on effects in terms of the identity of those who either choose to be categorised as disabled or are categorised in this way by others.

As a result of anti-discrimination legislation, universities at one level buy into an understanding of disability as a political category and an important equality strand, and have responded to legislative requirements prohibiting discrimination and requiring positive action to facilitate the participation of disabled students. The views of individual lecturers, however, reveal that not everyone subscribes to this liberal stance, and particularly in vocational fields of study questions continue to be raised about whether disabled people can ever be deemed fit to practise in areas such as education. Until very recently in Scotland, notions of an absolute standard of physical and mental fitness were underlined by the professional regulatory body requirement for a medical examination to rule out unfit individuals. The GTCS differs from professional regulatory bodies in other parts of the UK in its decision to scrap the fitness to practise standards. However, the attitudes of some university lecturers and school teachers discussed earlier indicate that it will be some time before the implications of this decision are fully understood by the teaching profession.

The case studies in this chapter are of students with unseen or almost unseen impairments, by far the largest group of disabled students in higher education. At school, Jean learnt that additional support may be helpful, but such needs were inherently shameful and must be hidden from other members of the class. At university, a doctor carrying out a medical examination intended to weed out the unfit from teaching suggested that she might benefit from a diagnosis of dyslexia in order receive certain benefits and allowances. Following a psychological examination, Jean was rewarded for the new diagnosis, receiving the Disabled Students Allowance, allowing her to purchase a laptop computer and to benefit from extra time in examinations. The downside, however, came in the form of institutional pressure to disclose her diagnosis on her school placement, risking the disapproval of teaching staff and possible damage to her future employment prospects. Unsurprisingly, Jean experienced considerable conflict as a result of these pressures, and by the end of the study had decided to jettison the category of disability as a significant part of her identity, since in the workplace it appeared that the disbenefits outweighed any benefits. Her judgment appeared to be shared by the vast majority of disabled students moving into their induction year, where less than a third of students who were identified as disabled at university chose to disclose a disability on making the transition into working life.

Andrew's experience was slightly different. Like Jean, he was acutely aware of the stigma associated with being identified as disabled and the possible resentment of other students towards someone who appeared to be getting additional help. As a result, Andrew generally tried to pass as non-disabled, disclosing his impairment only to a small group of trusted friends and lecturers. However, the experience of failing to disclose an impairment on placement made him realise that in some situations he might need the protection of the law in order to obtain reasonable adjustments. In general, the case studies of Andrew and Jean reveal the powerful pressures which prevent students from disclosing an impairment when they move into the workplace, and the realities of ongoing prejudice in both universities and schools.

A final note

Fitness to teach standards and requirements still exist in England and were recently revised (DfES, 2007). They exist alongside guidance to ITT providers on disability discrimination and fitness to teach (TDA, 2007) which are intended to encourage fair decisions in selecting disabled potential trainees. The existence of the Training and Development Agency for Schools (TDA) guidance is recognition of tensions between equality legislation and fitness to practise standards and a need to change historical attitudes towards impairment as a bar to teaching. Individual ITT providers nevertheless continue to interpret the standards in their own way (Beverton and Riddick, 2008). Although the notion of 'fitness to practise' has been discarded as an entry requirement to teaching in Scotland, on the grounds that it is anachronistic and discriminatory, it clearly continues to exist in people's minds, reinforcing the idea of disability as individual deficit and the disabled individual as unworthy of full social inclusion. This means that the situation may not be so very different in Scotland and England, and the dilemmas facing Andrew and Jean in Scotland are likely to be shared by trainees in England.

Chapter 8

Troublesome transitions?

Disabled students' entry into and journey through higher education

Elisabet Weedon and Sheila Riddell

Transitions in and out of education and training are part of the life-long learning agenda as citizens are now expected to engage in learning throughout the lifespan (Scottish Executive, 2003; Field, 2006). Traditional higher education students will have experienced at least five transitions in their initial learning career, from first entry to school to leaving higher education. Non-traditional students may experience more transitions or find the transitions harder to cope with, for example, due to lack of knowledge and awareness of the norms and values of higher education (Lang and Robinson, 2003). Universities have also transformed considerably having changed from being institutions for a small elite to catering for a much wider range of students. Universities are now managed differently which includes target setting in relation to widening participation (see e.g. Riddell, Tinklin and Wilson, 2005). While targeting and benchmarking offer one way of examining whether universities are increasing provision for disadvantaged groups it does not provide insights into the educational experiences of disadvantaged groups, including how they cope with transitions. This chapter examines the transition experiences of disabled students focusing on the following questions:

- What are the students' experiences of transition into, passage through and exit from university?
- What, if any, differences are there between students with different impairments?
- According to students' perceptions and experiences, how is the process managed by the university and others?
- What constitutes and contributes towards a successful transition or successful transitions, for whom is it 'successful'?

Conceptualisations of transitions

Ecclestone stresses that the concept of transitions is problematic and that research into transitions is fragmented and lacking in conceptual clarity (Ecclestone, 2007a). She identifies three main perspectives, the first exemplified by Lam and Pollard (2006). Their work focuses on children's entry to kindergarten and it draws on conceptualisations using a 'rites of passage' approach augmented by sociocultural theory. In a review of previous research they note that others have described transitions as the movement between different institutional settings and also referred to types of transitions as either horizontal or vertical. The term vertical transition denotes movement between programmes or agencies over time; horizontal transitions occur within the same time frame but from one setting to another. In terms of students, vertical transitions could be viewed as movement from school to higher education or from one year to the next. Horizontal transitions could encompass movement from university to work or home, or within the university from formal learning setting to informal learning. Lam and Pollard (2006) note that much of the research has focused on transitions between contexts but they also state that later studies have considered shifts in identity such as 'child' at home and 'pupil' in kindergarten. In the higher education context this could imply change in identity from 'pupil' at school to 'student' at the university; between 'employee' at work and 'student' or 'parent' at home to 'student' at the university.

The impact of transitions on identity is emphasised to a greater extent by the second perspective outlined by Ecclestone. This approach is exemplified in research on learning careers such as that of Bloomer (2001), Bloomer and Hodkinson (2000) and Gallacher et al. (2002). Bloomer notes that to understand the choices a student makes in order to become and continue as a student it is essential to take into account structural factors such as gender, family background and ethnicity. In addition, he sees educational experiences and attainments and institutional cultures as being of importance (Bloomer, 2001). The concept of a 'career' in the non-traditional sense was developed by the Chicago school of sociologists and adapted into the concept of 'learning career' which has been used mainly to explore the experiences of students in further education, both younger learners (Bloomer and Hodkinson, 2000) and more mature learners (Gallacher et al., 2002). Gallacher and colleagues developed the concept further to take into account the experiences of individuals who were re-engaging with learning after a break. They distinguish between the impact of individual and institutional factors and argue that both play a role in an individual's developing learning career and can lead to a change in identity. From this perspective transitions into an educational context contribute to changes in social identity over a period of time.

A third approach, stemming from post-modernist views, sees life as a process of transitions. This perspective, according to Ecclestone, questions the notion that there is a single entity that can be transformed. Rather, people have multiple identities which are affected by social structures such as class and gender. It also questions the extent to which individuals can create coherent narratives about themselves which demonstrate a chronologically ordered development of a particular identity and argues instead for multiple identities based on unconscious and sometimes contradictory influences. From the perspective of disabled students this may mean an identity as a higher education student but also as disabled. The nature of an impairment will vary in its impact. For example, a student with epilepsy may have no problems when the condition is successfully controlled but if there is a change it can have a considerable impact. (Issues of identity are also discussed in chapters 6 and 7.)

These three perspectives reflect different assumptions about the relationship between identity, agency and structure which, in the case of the third perspective is more difficult to disentangle. According to Ecclestone (2007b), one thread running through these writings is that of transitions as problematic and requiring to be managed. She argues that this can lead to the construction of 'fragile identities' that cannot cope with the demands of education without support from professionals. The transitions of the case study students will now be examined, first through a brief overview including all the students and then by looking in more detail at two of the students.

Transitions and the student group

Earlier research has shown that disabled students did less well than non-disabled students in overall outcomes (Riddell et al., 2005). While this is still the case for the students in Universities 1 and 3 (see chapter 1 for a description of the universities), the overall trend shows that disabled students are doing slightly better, and in University 2 there was no difference between disabled and non-disabled students. (There were no statistics comparing outcomes for disabled and non-disabled students in University 4.) It seems that transitions are more problematic for at least some of the disabled students in relation to achieving a satisfactory transition out of the university. (For an overview of the case study students see Appendix A.1.)

Transitions into university pose additional challenges for disabled students in relation to disclosure. In University 1 all 14 case study students disclosed a disability on their application form but not to the Disability Office which is needed to trigger any adjustments required. According to the Disability Office, in this university around 70–75 per cent of those who have disclosed on entry make contact with them. As can be seen later from the individual case studies, some students assumed that disclosure on the application form triggered adjustments, an assumption shared by other students in this study (see chapter 3; Fuller, Bradley and Healey 2004; Fuller *et al.*, 2004). Of the 14 students 3 did not complete their intended degree and 1 of these students had three attempts initially at getting started with the course.

In University 3 there were four students; two with dyslexia, one had dyspraxia and one with hearing loss. The student with hearing loss withdrew from the course, while the other three completed, two with upper and one with lower second class degrees. The first three were regularly contacted by the Disability Office but the student with hearing loss was not contacted although teaching staff were aware of her impairment. In University 3, two of the eight students had not completed the course by the end of the project. One, a dyslexic student, withdrew and the other who was mobility impaired took a year. In University 4 two of the five case study students made slow progress as they repeated a year.

This overview of all the case study students suggests that transitions are experienced differently by students with different impairments. Overall there is a suggestion that those with unseen impairments, excluding students with dyslexia and dyspraxia, are most at risk. This will be discussed further under emerging themes, drawing on all the case study students.

The majority of students did not view themselves as disabled; however, in order to access necessary support the students needed to take a pragmatic approach and use the label. Some struggled with this as they considered it a negative label. Older students such as Jean and Barry felt it identified them as 'remedial', a term that had been used at school to single out those who were learning impaired. For Jean 'disabled' became a 'transitory' label which she used throughout her university career to access some extra time in exams and technological support; however she discarded it when entering the labour market.

Findings: Teresa and Alan

This section examines transitions in greater depth from the perspective of two students in University 1. Teresa and Alan have been selected because they have 'unseen' impairments which adds an extra dimension in relation to disclosure: epilepsy in the case of Teresa and multiple impairments in the case of Alan. Both had enrolled for standard four-year honours degree programmes and had identified themselves as disabled on the application form. The experiences of two other students at this university, one with a visible impairment and one with mental health problems, have been explored elsewhere (see Weedon and Riddell, 2007b).

Teresa

Teresa, a mature student who studied Bioscience, had epilepsy which started in early childhood but was undiagnosed until she was 18. She suffered from bad migraines, one aspect of epilepsy, throughout her school life but was considered as 'skiving' by the head teacher in her private school. She was an intrinsically motivated student who described the most positive aspect of being a student as the education, the learning and being part of a team that was learning. She did not consider herself disabled but did not mind telling people about her epilepsy which she saw as a medical condition.

At the beginning of her course she hoped to carry on to post-graduate research. Her initial transition into the university seemed unproblematic but she assumed that disclosing her impairment on the application form would automatically alert relevant staff to her condition:

> I didn't [contact the Disability Office]. I assumed that . . . when I first came to the university, they give you all of these papers to sign and . . . so I did tick a bright red box that said 'you are disabled' and I assumed that because I had done that and on [the] Student Portal, they had me down as unseen disability, I assumed that that was on my file for my Director of Studies and all of the course organisers to know. But it wasn't, so I got myself into trouble for not saying at the beginning that I had these problems.
>
> (Teresa)

Her migraines remained a problem, leading to her missing lectures and deadlines. As staff were not aware of her impairment she spent a lot of time seeking extensions and having to provide a doctor's note to support her case. She finally contacted the Disability Office towards the end of her second year which improved her support considerably. She completed Years 1 and 2 successfully and progressed into third year. We lost contact with her at this point and did not speak to her again until a year later. It turned out that her headaches had got worse and she had taken a year out, as she put it 'to sort herself out'. She discussed this with her Director of Studies who was very supportive and made all the arrangements for her return. She did return to start third year again (of a four-year degree) but halfway through the year she had to withdraw finally from her course as she could not keep up with the lectures and the assignment deadlines. During the final interview it emerged that Teresa also had mental health difficulties and she was taking antidepressants. She had not realised that she was suffering from depression – she thought that the way she was feeling was a side effect of the drugs that she was taking for her epilepsy.

Teresa had a successful transition into the university; she was a very committed student and explained that she would miss her student identity when she left:

> Education, just being part of the group, I love being part of the group, wearing a university hoodie. That's what I am going to miss the most.
>
> (Teresa)

However, her transitions after second year and out of the university were not successful. She would have liked to continue part-time but her financial situation and lack of funding for part-time students made that impossible for her. As a mature student she did not want to draw on family support and whilst she referred to good friends, she did not seem to have a close support network in the area as she had moved flats several times and changed flatmates:

> Family no good, they try, they would be there if I reached out to them but it is just my own psychological problem that I can't do that . . . I just don't know how to, I just can't. I have issues there. But I do have good friends.
>
> (Teresa)

Alan

Alan entered university after completing his A-levels at a comprehensive school which he described as 'good'. He had multiple impairments – cystic fibrosis, diabetes and epilepsy – and was doing a BSc in Environmental Geoscience. Like Teresa, he disclosed his impairment on the application form, but did not make any contact with the Disability Office until the end of second year and was then given extra time in exams. His disclosure on the application form triggered access to disabled student accommodation. He assumed that this would mean that staff would be informed of his impairments:

> No, I haven't sort of . . . they are aware of me but . . . [I] haven't had a meeting 'do you need anything specific?' . . . I assume so [that DoS knows about it]. I have never discussed it with him. He must do, it's on the form.
>
> (Alan)

Transition into the university caused no difficulties but Alan was far more ambivalent towards his studies than Teresa – being a learner did not seem to be a key feature of his life. Like Teresa his main difficulties emerged at the end of the second year when he failed one of his exams. He described himself as a lazy student who did not apply himself properly. He does not see his impairment as having an undue influence on his studies but says that he has to spend about two hours every day doing physiotherapy. He was also concerned about using any of his impairments as an excuse:

> The CF [cystic fibrosis] doesn't really [impact] – it's just an extra couple of hours in the day, it doesn't impair learning at all. The diabetes, I think it is mainly concentration, sometimes if I get too high blood sugars then it is very hard to keep my mind focused on one thing . . . It is fairly hard to keep it at a critical level. It is quite tricky for me. But whether that is just an excuse for me not concentrating sufficiently I don't know.
>
> (Alan)

Alan suffered a serious medical problem shortly after starting third year, a brain tumour that he had had for some time had suddenly got larger and he had to go in for surgery. As with his other impairments he played down the impact:

Fairly major upheaval . . . I went down for a scan . . . they were concerned that it was cancer. So they chopped me up, got it out, and it's fine!

(Alan)

This interruption to his studies led to him missing out the first semester of Year 3. He returned in Semester 2 completed the required modules over the next year, finishing at Christmas with an ordinary degree. During this period he participated in a fieldwork trip where he was given conflicting messages, one member of staff suggesting he might be able to complete his honours degree; however, he had problems discussing this with his Director of Studies:

I am still not convinced that it is going to be as easy as [name] was saying. That I can just sort of walk in and do it . . . I'll wait and see . . . it is slightly annoying that my DoS didn't really consider that they could offer me special circumstances . . . I thought my DoS would be sort of more . . . a little bit more proactive. I don't expect them to do anything for me . . . just . . . [be aware of the possibilities]. He has just ignored my emails.

(Alan)

Alan finally settled for an ordinary degree and left the university and moved into temporary employment whilst examining his future options. In terms of transitions from school to university and into adulthood, Alan saw his university experience as positive but the main reason was not the learning and studying:

Just being out, looking after myself living independently – that seems to miss the point of being at university cause one's got to learn as well . . . I obviously have knowledge that I didn't have before. [I] probably have [learnt skills] but don't feel I can quantify that . . . it is such a drawn out process.

(Alan)

Throughout his interviews Alan stressed that he did not wish to see his impairment as an excuse though at the end he admitted that it may have had more of an impact than perhaps he had been willing to recognise. When summarising what he had found most difficult throughout his studies he focused on his lack of ability to really apply himself:

Really knuckling down and just having the will to just sit down and learn things properly, I really struggle, not so much with motivation, I really struggle with actually sitting down and concentrating and I would say maybe 10 per cent of that could be attributed to disability . . . diabetes is quite hard if blood sugar is high or low then you can't be concentrating . . . yeah so that is fair. You're always thinking is that an excuse to not applying yourself to a 2-hour block. That's more of an excuse . . . an excuse not to work.

(Alan)

These two students are similar in that they had unseen disabilities, declared on entry to the universities, both had relatively successful transitions into the university and for both the main problems started at the end of second year, the transition point into the honours course. Both left the university with a qualification below the one they had enrolled for. Alan stated that he was satisfied with this, whilst Teresa felt that she was a failure. They differed in the level of pastoral support as Teresa was well supported but Alan had problems in contacting his Director of Studies. Their impairment and attitude to it also differed. Alan was open and matter of fact about his impairments, whereas Teresa found it more difficult to discuss hers and only admitted her mental health difficulties to the research team towards the end of her studies.

Emerging themes

Transitions in, through and out of the university

Transitions into the university were unproblematic for the majority of the students in that they coped with the demands of their course in the early stages. The exception was one student with mental health difficulties who started twice before finally making a successful transition (Weedon and Riddell, 2007b). The main issue on entry centred on disclosure and making contact with the Disability Office. It is an additional difficulty for disabled students with unseen disabilities not experienced by non-disabled students. The lack of contact with the disability staff did not necessarily pose a problem initially; however, for many, it did translate into a problem on transition to a higher level such as the honours programme in universities with four-year degrees. Teresa experienced problems such as missing deadlines and lectures became more problematic. She spent a considerable amount of time persuading staff that she was entitled to an extension; however, this was not fully accepted until proper procedures were in place. Alan started to find it more difficult to achieve the grades required and in reflecting on his experiences at the end of his course wished that he, or the Disability Office had been more proactive at the beginning of his studies:

> For somebody like me . . . things like making every student when they declare a disability go to the Disability Office in the first, say, month, I don't know if that is possible, . . . but that would have been useful . . . you're a lot younger in the first year . . . I hadn't lived away from home, I hadn't been away from home. Similarly with your DoS – to say 'I see you are registered disabled – let's talk about it'.
>
> (Alan)

Teresa had adopted a strong student identity and her transition into becoming a student was a central part of her life. Her early exit from the university therefore impacted greatly on her identity and the learning career she had intended to develop, which left her without alternative plans for the future. Alan on the other hand had not adopted a strong student identity; it was more important to him that he could live independently away from home. In a sense this suggests a 'rites of passage' transition as identified by Lam and Pollard (2006). For younger students then, there is a shift to becoming an adult and defining what is your own responsibility and that of others is an issue, for example in relation to managing successful transitions.

A further challenge is presented by transitions between the university and the workplace when students' courses included placements or study abroad. There was variation between the universities in terms of assisting teacher training students with disclosure when on placement. One teacher training student, Jean, with dyslexia found disclosure when on placement problematic (see chapter 6), and another, Lesley, encountered access difficulties because the school had not been informed of her impairment. A mobility impaired student, Karrie, experienced difficulties in finding a personal assistant for her compulsory year abroad placement resulting in her father accompanying her (see chapter 3 for more discussion of placements). These students all came from University 1: it is not clear how supportive the other universities may have been as none of the students in these universities were involved with exchange or placement abroad.

Differences between students with different impairments

Our research suggests that the impact of transitions was affected by a student's type of impairment. Those with very visible impairments such as mobility impairment or wheelchair use had support in place from the start which smoothed entry into and through the university. Dyslexic students, with the exception of Ben, also had support put into place early and were in receipt of Disabled Students' Allowance (DSA). Overall the outcomes for dyslexic students differed little from non-disabled students, indicating that the level of support provided within the university ensures these students make effective transitions. There was an indication of delays in the early stages of the courses due to assessment requirements; however, once support was in place the students coped well at later transition stages.

Transitions, both into and within the university, caused greater problems for students with other types of unseen impairments and universities seemed less aware of these students and the difficulties they faced. The evidence from Alan and Teresa shows this quite clearly. In particular, students with mental health difficulties are, based on our research, the most vulnerable. Teresa was unwilling to accept her mental health problems until later on and did not disclose it to the university, another student, Euan, felt that mental health difficulties were not considered a 'disability'. He therefore did not disclose it initially and experienced considerable difficulties at the beginning, settled into study, but failed to reach his initial goal of obtaining an honours degree.

Institutional management of transitions

On entry to university students requiring support need to be in contact with the Disability Office and, where relevant, this leads to an application for the DSA. The four universities varied in terms of initial contact with the students. University 2 claimed to contact all who had disclosed their disability on the application form; however, one of the case study students had not been contacted. The students had relatively few complaints about this process. However, the main complaint, that the process was slow, meant for some that support was not in place until the second year of their studies, with obvious detrimental effects (see chapter 3 for more on the process of application to DSA).

Students with unseen disabilities, excluding those with dyslexia, clearly posed a greater challenge for the universities. Students with mental health issues found disclosure highly problematic; out of the three students (Euan, Teresa and Cara) with this difficulty, only one disclosed. Euan was provided with effective support, but nonetheless did not manage to complete his intended course. Students with epilepsy also experienced considerable difficulties. Teresa had disclosed her epilepsy as had another student, Dermot. While both indicated that the Disability Office was supportive they failed to complete their course.

Students with an unseen disability face having to decide whether to disclose it or not. Even for students with dyslexia this was an issue, especially for those who had received little support from their school. Once diagnosed and accepted as 'dyslexic students' their support was generally well managed by their university mainly through the use of standardised adjustments such as extra time in exams or extensions for coursework assessments and these students coped well. This is evidenced by the results for this group of students: of the fourteen students only one withdrew from the course and two achieved first class honours degrees. The main area of difficulty experienced by some of these students was transition to the workplace for practical placements.

However, for students with other unseen impairments the experience was not as satisfactory. This could be due to the nature of the support required. The main support for dyslexic students was in terms of standardised adjustments or equipment purchased through DSA. Students with epilepsy may experience far more variation in the extent to which their impairment impacts on their studies and this is also likely to be the case for students with mental health difficulties. This is more difficult to tackle with routine, standardised approaches to reasonable adjustments. Pastoral care and support, while important for all students, is likely to be particularly so for this group of students. Students with an unchanging impairment such as hearing loss may feel compelled to disclose it because their condition, unlike some other unseen impairments, requires constant reasonable adjustments. For some students their impairment may lead to sensitivity to different teaching environments. A hearing impaired student, for example, has to make their own adjustments in the transition between a lecture theatre with a hearing loop to a tutorial room with possibly poor acoustics, and between staff who routinely wear a microphone to make themselves heard and those who are reluctant to do so.

Universities have made strides in managing transitions for students with impairments; however, the issue over disclosure on entry to the university is still problematic. The extent to which students require encouragement to disclose and whose responsibility that is, is likely to continue as an issue. In addition, our research suggests that developing effective support mechanisms for students with non-standard requirements requires attention. This seems particularly important for students with mental health difficulties as a recent report noted that this group of students were particularly vulnerable at periods of transition (Stanley, Mallon et al., 2007) but also for students with other unseen impairments such as epilepsy.

What constitutes a successful transition?

For the university, it could be argued, successful transitions are those that are not problematic on entry, show reasonable progress through a particular programme of study and end with the conferment of a degree which leads to employment or further studies. It would be considered particularly successful if the outcome is a first and is achieved in the minimum time available for that particular programme. Applying that criterion to University 1, Jean and James can be considered highly successful; eight of the others were successful as they had either completed their degree or were on track to do so; four are more problematic. Lesley is perhaps the easiest to account for as she had taken a year out due to a non-academic transition, pregnancy, and was intending to return. Euan and Alan obtained an ordinary degree having hoped to achieve honours. Teresa was awarded a Diploma in Higher Education after two years of study although she had also intended to do an honours degree.

The ordinary degree, as an alternative to honours degrees, has existed for some time but the certificate and diploma are more recent and linked to the development of an accreditation framework. The intention is to allow for easy credit transfer between universities and open up opportunities for students to continue studying at a later stage. Their existence allows the university to classify exits at a particular level as 'successfully completed' rather than as a 'drop out'. From the institutional perspective then, the transitions for most 31 students were successful, apart from the two who withdrew from their course without qualification (Divina, Dermot).

However, students may not see it in the same way. Looking in more detail at three of the students shows that Euan fought the university's decision not to allow him onto the honours part of the course vigorously but unsuccessfully. In the end he decided to agree to the ordinary degree option and work on developing a career in IT. When last in contact he had been shortlisted for an IT job and, in his final interview, he stressed the personal development and skills that his time at university had provided. This would suggest a transition in identity from that as a student towards that of a working adult. If Euan is successful in gaining employment he is doing well in comparison with other students with mental health difficulties. According to the Association of Graduate Careers Advisory Services (AGCAS) data, graduates with mental health difficulties had greatest difficulties in securing employment, with only 36.7 per cent of students in this category being able to find work in 2005 (AGCAS, 2007). Euan had not managed to attend school in his last year because of panic attacks, whereas in his last year at university he was able to attend without extra support. Clearly he had changed during this period in a positive way and that in a sense could be considered a successful transition from a school pupil into becoming a student and towards an identity of an adult with work. This aspect of his success results from the university providing him with effective support in the early stages of his university career and may also attributed to the provision of considerable parental support throughout.

Alan also had his intended university career cut short but had made a successful transition into temporary work that would provide experience towards the kind of future career that he hoped to develop. He saw his university experience as providing an effective transition from depending on parents to living independently. Teresa's situation was far less satisfactory. She did not speak of any opportunities for work and had managed to get by in her year out by living very frugally and earning some money dog-walking. Her transitions through (after the second year) and out of the university can therefore be considered unsuccessful for her in spite of her exiting with a diploma.

The conceptualisations of transitions all include some focus on identity and changes in identity. The first approach (Lam and Pollard, 2006) described transitions as both horizontal and vertical and explored them as 'rites of passage'. They considered identity change during this process but not to the same extent as that of the learning career approach of Gallacher *et al.* (2002). The third approach argued that individuals do not have a single identity and that the process of shaping identity is not linear from one identity to another. It could be argued that these approaches are not mutually exclusive, for example the vertical transitions mentioned by the first approach could indicate that an individual posesses multiple identities and that the social context elicits a particular identity. However, this possibly disregards the fluidity of the post-modernist approach. In terms of explaining the students' transitions it could be argued that the 'rites of passage' approach does seem to encapsulate the experiences of many of the young middle-class students. The social aspect of the university experience is as important as the learning, though the students often mention the struggle of coming to terms with time management and not being cosseted to the same extent as at school. The learning career approach does not seem to offer a useful way of exploring the experiences of most of the younger students who came from a middle-class background straight to university. However, it potentially accounts for more of the older, mature and also the 'non-traditional' students' experiences. For example, Andrew stressed, at the end of his course, that his main identity was now as a professional teacher and that being both disabled and (a rare) *male* primary teacher was of less importance. This exemplifies what Ecclestone (2007a) refers to as 'becoming somebody' with the learning experience providing a transition between two states of 'being'. While this was also the case for Jean she, in addition, was juggling multiple roles – working-class student, mother, wife and daughter. At the end of the course she said that her greatest achievement was to get a degree but that she still felt that somebody might tell her she is a fraud because people from her background 'don't get degrees'.

Conceptualisation of transitions requires further examination and there is no single approach that can capture the transitions of disabled students; however, it does provide a useful mechanism for exploring at which point(s) in a student's career there may be particularly problematic transitions, points where additional support may be required.

To summarise, impairment has an impact on transitions throughout a student's university career. However, its impact varies according to type of impairment as well as age and social class of the student. Routine adjustments have been effective in smoothing transitions for some students but students with more complex needs, requiring more subtle adjustments, are still struggling. For many, the family provides additional support not offered by the university, and students who do not have access to such support may well be at particular risk. Most of the students play down the impact of their impairment and are, in some cases, unwilling to seek support to which they are entitled. Universities that see disclosure as a matter for the individual student face difficulties reaching out to some students.

Chapter 9

Organisational structures for disability support

Contradictions as catalysts for change

Jan Georgeson

Among the aims for the project was investigating across subject disciplines and institutional contexts the processes by which change occurs in teaching, learning and assessment and the relationship of these aspects of education to outcomes for disabled students. Four different types of university were specifically selected in order to investigate the comparability of experience across the university sector, with a view to developing case studies of the way disability issues and disabled students were treated in universities with different cultures.

In practice, the group of students recruited for the project was diffusely spread over subjects, so that a comparison based on discipline and institution was not viable. As we interviewed teaching and administrative staff, it also began to emerge that an analysis based on a simple distinction such as arts versus science subjects would not capture the complex ways in which processes to support disabled students had developed. This chapter then focuses on dilemmas and contradictions in one university to illustrate this complexity. The organisational structures to be considered are concerned with services, facilities and accommodations to provide disabled students with specific and generic support, and also with the decisions about who has access to these and the systems to communicate these decisions. Information about these organisational structures has been derived from interviews with academic staff who worked directly with the students followed in the project, and with administrative and academic staff who had responsibility for the organisation or management of disability provision. Relevant documents such as policies and guidance manuals were also examined and questions relating to support structures were included in the interviews with students over three years. All of these sources have informed the analysis which underpins this chapter.

The organisational structures that are in place in the four universities embody each institution's response to successive waves of guidance and legislation that have laid out the requirements for higher education institutions with respect to disabled students. But they also incorporate strategies and procedures which have evolved over time in response to individual cases. Therefore, although each institution will have agreed on their overall strategy about how to carry out the business of disability support, what actually happens on the ground will have been shaped by everyday practices which have evolved *ad hoc* to meet student need.

We have found that disability provision in reality is the result of a complex interweaving of different motivations, at the institutional, departmental and individual level. At the institutional level, the advent of disability rights into a culture of accountability and a general inclination in society towards litigation, can sometimes give rise to an attitude of mere compliance, with staff supporting disabled students because they have to, in the same way that they have to comply with health and safety regulations. But there can also be strong motivation to support disabled students because it is generally held to be the morally right thing to do; that this is the kind of way we behave in this society, whether this springs from a strong social model motivation – 'we ought to remove barriers that society has erected which are limiting participation by all' – or out of something more akin to a charity/personal tragedy model – 'let us kind people do something to alleviate the lot of these poor unfortunates'. We have also occasionally detected motivation underpinned by the belief that providing support for disabled students is pedagogically the right thing to do; that thinking about how best to support disabled students leads to ways of teaching and assessment which are better for all students (see chapters 3 and 4). In many interviews with lecturers and other university staff, however, it became apparent that their personal experience of disability in themselves, their family, students or colleagues became a powerful source of motivation to provide support for disabled students. Admittedly, it was also true that in a few cases personal experience of teaching disabled students made some lecturers more reluctant subsequently to provide extra support for them (see later quotation from Lecturer Black).

The complexity of these competing motivations acting on different aspects of disability support within an institution can be explored using concepts derived from Activity Theory (Engeström, 1987), which have already been used effectively to explore the more specific issue of learning technologies and disabled students in higher education (Scanlon and Issroff, 2005). Disability support in each institution can be considered as an activity system, a network of purposeful actions towards recognised goals, underpinned by the shared overall motive to support disabled students along the trajectory of their chosen course. This will be shaped by the specific constraints and affordances of that particular institution and it is essential to think of such systems as multi-voiced; the standpoint of an administrator might be different from that of a lecturer or a member of the senior management team. It is therefore likely that, while the system as a whole might be working on support for disabled students, individuals within the system might focus on different aspects of student experience.

In the case of a diffuse system like disability support, Activity Theory offers a useful heuristic device to analyse what is happening at different levels of disability support and to carry out more detailed investigation into how people within the system perceive the object, or problem space, that they are working on. Analysing disability structures as activity systems is consistent with an approach underpinned by a social model of disability. Just as activity systems are understood as having been constructed over time in response to prevailing conditions, a social model of disability envisages barriers as having been erected over time by society in response to the needs of the non-disabled, but without sufficient awareness of the way these barriers constrain participation by those with impairments.

University 4 will be used to illustrate how organisational structures for disability support might operate as a system. This is illustrated in Figure 9.1 using a triangle format to illustrate the relationship between different aspects of provision.

The university had four linked elements to provide support for disabled students – centrally organised services, decision-making bodies/procedures, a system for transferring information about these decisions and services to staff and students, and reasonable adjustments which impacted directly on teaching and assessment.

Services were provided by the central Disability Office, which was managed through Student Services and provided advice to students through Disability Advisors with responsibilities for specific kinds of disability. Students had most contact with these advisors during the process of applying to and entering the university, including applying for Disabled Students' Allowance (DSA) and setting up support, such as personal dyslexia tutors and note-takers. The Disability Advisory Team, in conjunction with Human Resources, also had responsibility

Tools – What is being used?
Conceptual: University ethos of widening participation, strong links with workplace, maintenance of standards, assessment of need, level of disclosure, reasonable adjustments, special arrangements for exams
Human: Professional assessors, personal support assistants, notetakers, personal dyslexia tutors, technical support officers
Material: Buildings (Victorian and new-build), labs, workshops, halls, lifts, disabled parking places, hearing loops, forms, databases, dyslexia-alert stickers, handouts, WCT, websites

Subjects: Whose perspective?
All university staff who are involved in supporting or arranging support for disabled students

Object: What are people working on?
Students who meet the DDA definition
Motive: To achieve what? To enable disabled students to take full part in university life

Rules/values/norms: What supports or constrains the work?
- tradition/reputation for widening participation must be maintained
- tradition/reputation with industry for providing vocational training must be maintained
- SENDA made it illegal to discriminate against disabled students in the provision of education, training and other related services
- DDA defines what counts as disabled: some services/facilities are restricted to students who meet DDA definition
- DSA places limits on amount of money that can be spent on support for individual disabled students
- no extra time is allowed for submission of coursework, unless extenuating circumstances have been agreed upon
- nature of subject constrains participation by some disabled groups (esp. visual impaired)
- concern for maintenance of academic standards limits flexibility on modes of assessment/ type of adjustment/support
- part-time hourly paid staff are limited in their opportunities to take part in disability training
- administrative staff are limited in how much they can 'chase' academic staff to fulfill monitoring duties

Community: Who else is involved?
- all undergraduate and postgraduate students and their families
- all academic staff
- all administrative, technical, support, catering, maintenance staff
- local community
- schools (UK and worldwide)
- employers
- local and national government

Division of labour: How is the work shared?
- disabled students choose level of disclosure; apply for DSA, take disability assessments; attend classes, submit work, do exams, take part in social life of university
- academic staff make reasonable adjustments to their teaching/assessing
- departmental contacts pass on information about students and reasonable adjustments
- faculty coordinators monitor and advise university about disability issues
- advisory/review groups collate information, monitor, discuss, advise on disability policy planning, make decisions
- administrative staff collect and disseminate information and materials
- disability advisors provide information/advice and arrange support/training
- local community provides students with accommodation, services
- local authorities administer DSA
- employers provide work placements and jobs for graduates
- schools advise pupils on process of applying to university

Figure 9.1 Activity system analysis of organisational structures supporting disabled students at university

for staff development in relation to disability. Provision of support with specialised learning resources was also provided centrally via a special unit managed by library services.

There were also central groups with responsibility for disability policy and planning. The Disability Advisory Group was chaired by the Head of Student Affairs, who was a member of the university's Senior Management Team. The Disability Advisory Group collated information, monitored, discussed and advised the university on all aspects of policy and policy implementation in relation to disability. The Disability Review Panel would make recommendations to the Disability Advisory Group on support arrangements for disabled students or those with learning difficulties. The latter was an *ad hoc* panel convened to make decisions about specific cases which fell outside established practice.

Links between these central services and policy/planning bodies and what actually happened at the chalkface (or whiteboard) were made by means of academic staff who took on extra responsibility for disability issues in their faculties and within their departments. Each faculty had a named coordinator who worked with named contacts in academic departments. A similar pattern operated in services such as admissions and examinations, where the links were made directly with Disability Office. The Faculty Coordinators were all members of the Disability Advisory Group and could also serve on the Disability Review Panel. They were therefore involved mainly in strategic and extraordinary decisions about disability. The Departmental Disability Contacts, on the other hand, were more involved in how information about individual disabled students reached staff in their own departments and offered a point of contact in their department for both staff and students regarding disability issues.

Disability support at University 4 therefore operated using a radial network of 'local' faculty and departmental contacts to link central services and decision-making bodies to the staff and students. This mirrors a recently introduced strategy at University 4 developed after the project cohort moved through the university to address problems over who gets to know what about a student's needs. Coordinators of Adjustment have been introduced into each school who, with the delegated authority of the Head of School and acting on information distributed by the student's personal academic contact, decide the adjustments to be made to the academic processes in that School for each disabled student, and oversee their implementation through an Adjustments Schedule.

At University 4, the simplicity of the local enactment of centrally defined strategy masked considerable complexity when played out across the very different departments, and sometimes led to tensions or confusions. Some of these difficulties amount to contradictions. An activity system is characterised as constantly working through contradictions within and between its elements and this contributes to the way the system develops over time: 'New qualitative forms of activity emerge as solutions to the contradictions of the preceding form. This in turn takes place in the form of "invisible breakthroughs", innovations from below' (Engeström, 2004: online).

These contradictions can occur at different levels within the system, or as a result of something new (such as new regulations or new technology) coming into the system from outside. Whether the contradictions result in development will depend on the extent to which they are recognised by the system. Scanlon and Issroff have identified a basic contradiction in higher education: 'The primary contradiction in higher education activity takes the form of the student as person to be educated versus student as source of revenue and profit' (2005: 433).

This issue was often mentioned by our participants and proved to be a particular dilemma in the case of disabled students, because making reasonable adjustments often required finding more funding:

> I think one of the problems that education faces as a whole, is that since we're all working on income-led models, anything like responding to the DDA and making sure that people with disabilities are well catered for, tends to take a backseat, because we're told that what we need to do is get in as many students as possible and do as little work as possible to get the fees from them. And I know staff at the chalkboard may not take that attitude, but the institution as a whole is forced to do that. It's just one of the problems with the way education is funded at the moment. The inhibition towards making reasonable adjustments is finding the money; there's always some funding involved.
>
> (Lecturer Bryant)

In the following sections, further contradictions that emerged from analysis of data from University 4 will be described and ways in which these contradictions might surface and be resolved will also be considered.

Contradiction concerning concepts about disability within a department

This first example concerns an underlying contradiction between core elements of the university's ethos when applied to disabled students, which remained unresolved because of the organisational structure of one particular department. The resulting discrepancies were apparent only to the students, and they attributed these to differences in the personalities of staff, rather than to a fundamental contradiction between core values. This department was made up of a number of small, close-knit groups, supported by several part-time staff who were present on campus during student contact time and worked elsewhere the rest of the time. These part-time staff members were generally unable to attend training or other departmental or institutional events, which would have taken place in their own time. There was therefore scope within the department for staff to hold different views, but not much opportunity for them to discuss these.

University 4 has a longstanding tradition of widening participation as part of its core values, and for some staff this meant that they expected their department to respond positively to disability issues:

> There's a kind of ethos generally speaking of inclusivity. So when I distribute information about students, having a special need, generally speaking it will be received sympathetically ... [University 4] has a very positive attitude towards special needs students, it does attract more ... We've a reputation, for students with special needs, and consequently loads of other students will definitely be attracted to the course.
>
> (Lecturer Brooks)

The university also had a long history of providing vocational training, and courses were often delivered by tutors with recent or continuing experience of work in industry and commerce. This affected their approach to supporting students with additional needs. While not unsympathetic, they nonetheless expected students to use their own efforts to find ways of overcoming their difficulties, on the grounds that they would then be better prepared for the harsh reality of the workplace. These lecturers therefore recognised that there were barriers to students' access to the course, but placed responsibility on students themselves to overcome these barriers:

I come from industry, so I've got strong feelings in many ways about this whole set up. I give personally all the assistance I can to disabled students. When they come to me with their certificates, at the start of the year, the majority say 'I have a problem', and I turn round to them and say, 'you haven't got a problem at all, you've got a challenge. Rise to it'. And that's the way I work . . . I expect those students to play their part as well.

(Lecturer Butler)

This was connected to a concern that the degree obtained with support should have the same currency in the workplace, so that employers could rely on graduates having a certain level of competence, knowledge and skills:

I am looking at it not as a full time academic; I am looking at it from [the perspective of] a person who's had a life career in industry and commerce. I just have to be very careful, when I look at these degrees, that they have not been devalued as a result of over-support, over-pampering, just to get bottoms on seats for the next year. When they go and get the degree at the end of the year, every credit to them for doing it. But is it a true degree, or is it devalued when compared to somebody who's had to do it without all that extra support? For the one reason, that once they leave this establishment, they're on their own. And have they learnt that that support might not be quite available to the same degree, as they have enjoyed during their years at this university?

(Lecturer Butler)

The curriculum is determined by what we think is important in terms of educating and training people in a particular discipline and I do not think it is agreeable [to make the curriculum and assessment more accessible to disabled students]. Now one of the things people would say had happened is that the curriculum got easier because the students are less able, well that is a bad thing and I do not think that the curriculum should be subject to that sort of [adjustment].

(Lecturer Black)

Lecturers Brooks, Butler and Black clearly held different views but taught modules on the same course within this department. However, they had different experiences of disability and different roles within the department. Lecturer Brooks was disabled himself, Lecturer Butler had always worked part time in university and part time in industry, while Lecturer Black had had a career in industrial and university research. This resulted in students encountering different attitudes to their disability from staff, and different levels of support, which turned support into an interpersonal transaction, not a pedagogical contract. The student from our project who studied in this department learnt that a supportive staff attitude could not be taken for granted. This contributed to the impression that adjustments were something that could happen if he was dealing with a staff member who had 'friendly attitude, just willing to help' – not because adjustments were part of a considered response to his learning needs.

> I suppose if people know [that you're dyslexic] you get the extra time, you get the sympathy if you ask for it, a bit more understanding; if you just need a couple more days on an assignment or something you generally get it, if you don't push your luck presumably ... [Most of the academic staff have supported me] superbly. They understand, they're willing to flex a little bit and if you ever need help just appear at their office and they're always willing to give some help ... But in one subject a lecturer was quite unhelpful. He was just unwilling to help, unwilling to support, to advise ... this guy was very flat, it was really soulless, very impersonal. He wasn't very warm ... very icy.
>
> (Brandon)

This had the effect of positioning the disabled student as reliant on the sympathy and helpfulness of staff, thereby perpetuating a personal tragedy/charity model of disability, with consequent effects on self-esteem.

Detailed analysis of interviews with some of the more supportive members of staff in this department revealed that their approach to disability support was infused with discipline-specific discourse; they got excited by their successes in tinkering with the support system to improve the student's output, in the same way that they enjoyed working out how to maximise response from the systems they lectured on. However, what was missing in this department was a forum for them to share this enthusiasm with their more sceptical colleagues, in terms that these colleagues would have understood. This was because, with the organisation of the department as it stood, the pockets of enthusiasm and success had few opportunities to meet and people rarely shared their positive experiences about disability support with the rest of the department, and the part-time staff still employed in industry had no opportunities for discussions like this at all.

Contradiction between departmental ethos and university regulations

This example concerns a department at University 4 that taught an artistic subject with a strong performance element. It emerged in an interview with a lecturer who taught one of the students from the project, that she found it difficult to reconcile her department's strongly held values of trust and individualism with the rules about the availability of some kinds of special treatment only for those students who had been designated disabled by central services. This department strongly endorsed a particular approach to its subject which deliberately explored every student's strengths and weaknesses, encouraged them to confront these weaknesses and to become accustomed to being able to draw on their strengths to deal constructively with criticism. This approach was adopted because, as well as benefiting from the exploration of human frailty, the students would need to be able to cope with:

> The rigour of our trade and the cruelness of it, they've got to be able to take criticism and they've got to be able to work to a very high standard.
>
> (Lecturer Brand)

The department therefore needed to promote a strong sense of trust among course members and staff, to enable the soul-searching to take place and encourage students to support and feel supported by each other.

This acknowledgement that everyone has weaknesses/difficulties that can be a source of inspiration as well as requiring support, in many ways provided the disabled student with a truly inclusive experience:

> So whereas other people talk about self-esteem in a really rather vague flimsy way, I think we deliver very, very real techniques of how you ensure that you manage your life in the way you want it to be ... I think because of that we hit head on disability and prejudice, and power, status, making people feel small – we talk a lot about if you constantly learn to make a comparison between

self and other where that leaves you. That's a deeply problematic way for learning. We work a lot around those sorts of skills and I think for the disabled student that makes a lot of sense

(Lecturer Brand)

The university had regulations about who could receive extra support, depending on whether they met the Disability Discrimination Act (DDA) definition of disability, which was assessed independently before certain types of support were authorised. This cut right across the trust and responsivity to individual need which the department sought to promote. The lecturer recalled a talented student who, she believed, would have benefited just as much from some of the services which Bella, a dyslexic student followed in our project, received, notably help to buy a computer and a personal tutor to help with essay writing:

And it breaks my heart that this kid has struggled for three years, she would have done so well with someone sat beside her to help her do her essay, and if she's not dyslexic, I don't know how, it's beyond me because she's the most dyslexic student I have ever seen . . . everything is upside down and backwards and flipped. So that upsets me that we don't get support for those kinds of students.

(Lecturer Brand)

The issue about who counts as dyslexic and therefore who has access to the 'goodies' (Lecturer Butler – see quotation below) of extra time in exams and personal computers emerged from interviews with lecturers in other departments too, but they were generally content to ascribe the problem to something to do with inadequacies of the assessment process; it was a sources of irritation to them, not a full-blown contradiction which compromised everything that the department was trying to achieve. In this instance, the contradiction could have been resolved by a move towards more generic learning support, and more flexibility in modes of assessment – something which this lecturer would have been happy to consider.

A university-wide contradiction within the division of labour

According to University 4's terms of reference, the role of Departmental Disability Contact (DDC) is to work with the Disability Advisory

Team, staff and students to ensure appropriate support for students with disabilities during admissions, induction, enrolment, teaching and assessment, be a contact in the department for disability issues, and work with the Disability Advisory Team to provide information and advice about:

- Legislation relating to disability in higher education
- Common needs of people with specific disabilities
- The policies, services and facilities for students with disabilities and learning difficulties at the university
- Anticipatory duty and individual reasonable adjustment
- University sources of specialist advice
- Monitoring disability issues and reporting to the Head of Department

This is a weighty list of duties, and consequently only those with considerable interest in disability issues, or who wanted to develop such an interest tended to take on the role of DDC (in addition to teaching and administration):

> A role came up and my boss thought I might be interested in it because my PhD is related to disabilities as well. And I kind of jumped at the chance because I thought I may as well do something I'm interested in than be lumbered with something I'm not.
>
> (Lecturer Bolan)

In practice, the main element of the DDC's role is to receive information from [Disability Services] about which students in their departments have registered with a disability, and pass this information on to staff, then act as a point of contact for staff or students who need more information about disability issues.

Those who were new to the job expressed the need for more contact with their fellow DDCs across the university, but the lines of communication ran between department and central services, not between departments. Interviews with DDCs who were not disabled themselves confirmed a need for opportunities to extend their knowledge of disability issues, and some had made contact informally:

> I went to see J [another DDC in the same faculty], looked at their

procedures and slightly tweaked the way J did it. J seemed to make sense from A to Z; her system made sense to me, so I thought 'I'll copy J's system', because I hadn't had any training.

(Administrator Burden)

The DDC operates in all the different departments and we could possibly learn from each other actually. I have never been to a meeting that's been specially fixed for department coordinators. I feel that I would be able to do my job better if I had more knowledge maybe of the matter and that obviously takes a lot of time learning about different disabilities, etc., keeping up to date with new research, because things change don't they; look at how dyslexic students were taught 20 years ago, it's not the same as they're taught now.

(Lecturer Bolan)

The local-to-centre radial lines of communication, and hierarchical organisational structure with only Faculty Disability Coordinators being involved in strategic and extraordinary decision making, meant that the staff charged with establishing frontline contact with staff and students were often the least powerful and sometimes the least knowledgeable elements in the chain of communication. As discussed earlier, some lecturers needed convincing that they should make reasonable adjustments to enable disabled students to access the curriculum. Some DDCs who were administrators, while believing they were doing a good job, felt they lacked authority when required to chase academic staff who had not responded to requests for support:

I did feel it was more of an admin-y role, than an academic role, although my personal opinion is that we need an academic and an administrator involved in a joint DDC role. I set up a system, and I went to the faculty coordinators for advice, because the one thing that confused me is I didn't get any training at all, in the beginning. Nobody sort of said, 'are you doing this? This is what you do'. I'll be completely honest, the general consensus of opinion was, it shouldn't be a clerical person who was doing the role, it should be an academic. So I was a bit [laughs] put out by that, because I put my all into it. I set up a system, I was contacting people, and I felt like I'd got a great little system going, quite proud of it, something I do separately for myself, so I didn't see why it had to be an academic, although now I can see that, to bring academics on board, we could do with some authority, which generally clerical staff don't have.

(Administrator Burden)

Other DDCs were disabled members of the academic staff, and some Faculty Disability Coordinators combined their role with being DDC for their department. These DDCs were very knowledgeable about disability issues, did not have a problem communicating with staff or students, but found the administrative side of the dual role very demanding and time-consuming. There was a mismatch therefore between the combination of knowledge, skills and status required for the role of DDC and the knowledge, skills and status of the individuals who found themselves in the role, which seemed to be expecting too much of any one individual. As the administrator quoted earlier suggested, the role of DDC perhaps needed to be shared between academic and administrative staff, with specific training and cross university meetings for staff with responsibilities for disability support at departmental level. Such a suggestion could have been conveyed upwards through the chain of communication to those with strategic responsibility for disability support provision, but this would have relied on relatively low-status individuals making their concerns known to their Faculty Coordinators, who did not realise that there was a problem.

Contradictions between rules about assessment

In our interviews with lecturers and DDC in University 4, the issue of assessment raised most contradictions between different systems within the institution. Staff who understood their responsibility to make reasonable adjustments for disabled students submitting assignments sometimes found their efforts clashed with central regulations about assessment. Assessment modes and criteria were supposed to be published in advance, but this appeared to contradict the need for flexibility to accommodate individual requirements:

We've just had a new regulation about to come out, which says that we're supposed to have written every assessment before the module starts, which sounds great in terms of quality but the reality is if I then get a student who's on special needs come in, I've got to start making adjustments, and the two principles are conflicting at that point, and I think somebody in the quality department hadn't thought through this. I mean never mind beforehand; a student's allowed to declare at any point, so I've got to retain flexibility in thinking about [assessment]. It'd be nice to have heard something 'yes, do this, but, we recognise this', but some of the thinking isn't very joined up.

(Lecturer Barton)

This echoed recurrent tensions between systems for maintaining standards and procedures within the disability support system for making reasonable adjustments, which was apparent in the first contradiction described earlier and was connected with a deeper suspicion about the motivations of those students who asked for adjustments to assessment and examination procedures. This suspicion was exacerbated by the remoteness of individual lecturers from the central systems that assessed disability and pronounced special arrangements for examinations:

'Disabled' can be a whole tranche of things really. Some of them try it on, without doubt, and they get no change whatsoever, if you know they are trying it on. There's a lot of goodies to be had, if you get enough marks on your medical checks.

(Lecturer Butler)

[Extra time] is an absolute scandal, almost as big a scandal as translating questions for deaf students. It is an absolute disgrace. They are translating things to make it easier for them to understand on the basis that their English is not their first language. The majority of our students have English as their second language and they do not get things made easier for them. Translating exams should not be allowed; extra time in exams should not be allowed.

(Lecturer Black)

The less visible the impairment, the more suspicions seemed to be aroused:

I have bad experiences with [dyslexic students] . . . I think that most dyslexics are faking it; I do not think they have any disability, they are just not that bright; . . . if they do not do well they say it's part of their dyslexia . . . I have students who have been assessed as having dyslexia whose work has been a bit odd in the way they present it but . . . who have really done well. Other students who claimed to have dyslexia . . . have made mistakes in programming and say 'I cannot do this because I have dyslexia'.

(Lecturer Black)

However, there was some evidence that staff were also starting to question the usefulness of the standard tools available to make examinations more accessible to disabled students. In the example below, the designated extra time proved to be a disadvantage to a student with Attention Deficit Hyperactivity Disorder (ADHD). This contradiction prompted the lecturer to work with the student to develop his exam technique, which resulted in a more successful approach:

> I think there's just this tendency that the reasonable adjustment is you give people 25 per cent extra time in exams or 50 per cent extra time in exams it seems to be quite blanket . . . and very early on, we started going through some of the tests that we'd done. What he was doing was that he was writing down all of the right answers, going back, looking at them, and crossing them out and starting again and writing down wrong answers. It was very specific to his learning difficulty and it was the attention deficit and hyperactivity that made him do that. So we came up with this sort of scheme, where he phased what he did in exams, and he didn't necessarily use the extra time.

(Lecturer Bryant)

Brandon reported similar dissatisfaction with the application of a standard tool for support for dyslexic students in exams. He had been allocated a reader, and the reader insisted on reading out all the questions, even though they were largely mathematical symbols and much easier to understand visually than verbally (see chapter 3 for Brandon's words).

There were many other examples which frustrated both students and staff alike where the rigidity of the rules surrounding examination and assessment procedures cut across the need for individual accommodations to make the processes accessible to all; some courses in computing-based subjects still insisted that all examinations had to be handwritten, and while extra time was available for written exams, it was not available for submission of examinable project work, even to students who had intermittent illnesses or time management problems:

Well, with dyslexics, if students do exams, they get an extra 25 per cent of time. But there's nothing in place for students doing practical projects. I think this isn't fair, given their problems with time management. The same is true for [performance] students with dyslexia, even for learning [their part].

(Administrator Bray)

It was clear that staff and students had ideas about how to make assessments and examinations more accessible, but sometimes found that this clashed with concerns to maintain standards. Because these tensions arose between systems and because of the difficulties with communication where problems had to be referred upward within systems, it was difficult for these issues to find their way to a forum where they could be debated. There were opportunities to debate matters concerned with teaching and learning; University 4 supported a thriving Pedagogic Research Forum, but this attracted a core group with a passion for pedagogic debate, rather than offering an open forum fed by the concerns of the wider teaching and administrative staff body.

Summary

It is often quoted (though seldom attributed) that making teaching more accessible to disabled students has the effect of making teaching better for all, and disabled students are sometimes cast in the role of catalysts for pedagogic change. In our interviews at University 4, staff and students certainly identified areas where they thought change was needed, and sometimes were able to work solutions out between themselves. This kind of change at an individual level can often lead to widespread change of the whole system:

In reality it always happens that a phenomenon which later becomes universal originally emerges as an individual, particular, specific phenomenon, as an exception from the rule [. . .] Thus, any new improvement of labour, every new mode of man's action in production, before becoming generally accepted and recognised, first emerges as a certain deviation from previously accepted and codified norms. Having emerged as an individual exception from the rule in the labour of one or several men, the new form is then taken over by others, becoming in time a new universal norm.

(Il'enkov, 1982: 83–4)

But in most instances here, solutions at an individual level were difficult to achieve, because staff and students were working not as individuals but as part of a network of the many systems that make up a degree course.

Activity Theory has its own procedures in the form of Development Work Research (DWR) that seek to reveal and resolve contradictions in organisations (Engeström, 1999), in which practitioners are guided to engage in reflective cycles of analysis, modeling and testing solutions. In DWR, the event that reveals contradictions within the system is the introduction of researchers from outside the setting, with the agreement by all involved to intensive engagement with the evidence of contradictions that the researchers lay before those who work within the system. This was not the kind of contract that we had established with the institutions in the project. While we recognised the need to provide feedback to each university as the research proceeded, we did this through a standing committee nominated by the Vice Chancellor, rather than through direct discussion with frontline staff.

Without an intervention such as DWR, a system must rely on its own processes to reveal contradictions and to agree to work on them. The inconsistencies that staff encountered at University 4 certainly prompted them to think about the way things were organised and how this could be more effective or fairer. However, the organisational structures and the system for communication within and between structures meant that the transformational potential of these emerging contradictions was often lost and change did not happen. In particular, there was a lack of opportunities for staff to learn 'horizontally' from each other about how to manage the processes of disability support, and for their views about organisational change to gather sufficient momentum to reach strategic levels. Some staff reported that they would welcome a forum for discussion of disability issues, both within and between departments. However, there was also evidence that such discussions needed to involve those members of staff who were more suspicious of the requirement to make reasonable adjustments. This points to the need for more widespread development opportunities for all staff, so that their support is underpinned by genuine conviction to inclusive ideals.

Part III

What are the implications of our study of disabled students' experiences?

Chapter 10

Reflections and conclusions

Mary Fuller, Sheila Riddell and Elisabet Weedon

Introduction

In this chapter we revisit the questions underpinning the study to summarise our main findings and, where appropriate, reflect on barriers we encountered in obtaining the information we sought. As a result of analysing material obtained from the institutional documents and two student surveys, interviews with disabled students and with teaching and other staff and observation of teaching sessions, there emerged a number of themes in addition to the research questions we started out with. These themes have been discussed in earlier chapters and together with the material from our research questions inform our conclusions about enhancing disabled students' learning and suggestions for further research, later in this chapter. Finally, we look at implications for further action and research aimed at enhancing disabled students' experience of teaching, learning and assessment in higher education.

Research questions revisited

We set out to document and analyse how disabled students experience teaching, learning and assessment during the course of their undergraduate studies in a variety of subjects and in four universities selected for their different histories and cultures. In addition we sought staff views about the ways in which disability and anti-discrimination legislation impinged on their working practices, particularly in relation to providing reasonable adjustments to teaching and assessment. Using the preceding chapters which investigated aspects of our research concerns we will present summary conclusions to the questions raised.

What are disabled students' experiences of reasonable adjustments to teaching, learning and assessment?

The emphasis in earlier chapters has been on how students obtained and experienced reasonable adjustments in their university courses and in work or other off-campus learning environments (see chapters 3, 4, 7 and 8 especially). Students' views of reasonable adjustments in teaching, learning and assessment can also be found in Fuller *et al.* (2004), Fuller, Healey and Bradley (2004), Healey *et al.* (2006) and Healey *et al.* (2008). Students' perceptions of support varied according to the subject studied, which university they attended and, possibly, their sense of entitlement. Dyslexic students at University 4, for example, the least socially advantaged institution with the least dedicated provision for such students, reported poorer access to some support such as lecture notes in advance. They also felt that lecturers were at times uncooperative. Students at University 1 who tended to come from more socially advantaged backgrounds were the most critical of the support they were given by lecturers, in spite of the fact that their general level of support seemed to be greater than in other universities.

In general, students' experience of adjustments was more positive in the higher education context than when they were on work placement where students sometimes found themselves in the middle of confusion between university department and workplace about whose responsibility it was to make and pay for adjustments. Students with unseen impairments studying Education found adjustments, and teacher attitudes to their impairment (see also Getzel, 2008), very variable. It was common for students to engage in multiple negotiations with different lecturers to ensure that agreements on reasonable adjustments were understood by them all. This is contrary to the spirit of the recent anti-discrimination legislation which requires anticipatory reasonable adjustments which should mean the need to negotiate individual adjustments is significantly reduced.

On the other hand some students considered their universities unnecessarily pushy, insisting on making adjustments or ordering equipment that the student did not want or use and there were some examples where an adjustment was not beneficial to a student (see also Fardell and Stead, 2008): for example, the routine extension of time for an examination which a student with Attention Deficit Hyperactivity Disorder (ADHD) found unhelpful. There were many examples of assistive technology taking too long to arrive, of failure to provide the student with sufficient training in its use and numerous experiences of the DSA process being slow.

Staff attitudes were a crucial aspect of the teaching and learning experiences for disabled students. The staff characteristics that students felt were most important were approachability, helpfulness, flexibility and being supportive, characteristics most likely to encourage students to disclose impairment(s) and learning needs. Students did not always find these congenial characteristics in their lecturers. That said, many students were happy with the adjustments which were made and appreciative of staff who met their expectations though many students were unhappy about having to accept the label of disability which was a pre-requisite for a request of an adjustment.

What are the learning and educational outcomes of disabled and non-disabled students?

University-wide records from the present study comparing retention and degree outcomes of disabled and non-disabled students were only available in three universities. Data for student intakes in 2001–02, 2002–03 and 2003–04 show that disabled students in Universities 1 and 3 (pre-1992 and post-1992 university, respectively) were more likely than non-disabled students to complete their course. Disabled students in University 2 (a pre-1992 institution) were now more likely to complete the course and to achieve better results than before so that there were no longer differences between disabled and non-disabled students in completion and degree outcomes. An earlier study using Higher Education Statistics Agency (HESA) statistics (Riddell *et al.*, 2005) showed that disabled students were slightly less likely to gain first and upper second class degrees and slightly more likely to gain third class degrees than non-disabled students. This picture still held true in Universities 1 and 3 where disabled students had poorer outcomes than non-disabled students in the same institution. Students in University 2 did better in terms of first class honours degrees, slightly worse in terms of upper seconds but overall the results of non-disabled and disabled students were quite similar.

The statistical data gathered by the institutions allowed only for a comparison between disabled and non-disabled students. Consequently we could not undertake the detailed analysis of retention rates and degree outcomes by impairment, or a cross-variable analysis of disabled students' social class, subject studied, gender or age as we had hoped and expected and which would have given this element of the research more depth. Disappointingly we are unable to comment in more detail from this retention and outcome data about where support seems to be effective and where more effective support is required.

Material from our case studies of disabled students in all four universities (see Appendix A.1) can throw some light on completion and degree outcome, though the numbers are too small to be more than indicative. There is complete data on 26 students: two of the original sample withdrew from the project so information is not available about completion or degree outcome. Three (10 per cent) did not complete their course, two of whom defined themselves as being middle class while the third left (to take up employment) before the point where students were asked about social class. By the end of the project two of the four 'older' students (aged 26 or more) had obtained a good degree (first or upper second) and two were yet to complete. Nineteen younger students had graduated (ten with a good degree), three had withdrawn and three were yet to finish. Seven of the thirteen students with dyslexia graduated with a good degree, four others graduated and two were yet to finish. Students with other unseen impairments, particularly those with fluctuating conditions such as mental health difficulties, did not perform as well: they were the least satisfied with their university experiences in general, expressed concern about disclosure of information about their impairment without their permission and were least likely to complete their courses. Indeed they were as likely to withdraw as to complete their course.

How do staff understand disability equality legislation in relation to teaching, learning and assessment?

Senior managers and disability support staff considered the Disability Discrimination Act provided a major impulse to institutional action. This was predominantly in the form of policy statements. They said relatively little about adjustments to teaching and assessment. Some lecturers and senior managers were concerned that putting reasonable adjustments in place might compromise academic standards and articulated their concerns especially in relation to students with dyslexia. In all four universities a considerable level of anxiety was evident partly to do with the cost of making adjustments, and partly to do with conferring unfair advantage on disabled students in comparison with other students who were having difficulty with their course. In summary staff were more exercised about what constituted 'reasonable' than about putting adjustments in place as such.

The quality assurance regime was resented by some staff in the two pre-1992 institutions (see chapter 2) and since the Research Assessment Exercise (RAE) was seen in these universities as a major policy driver, focusing staff attention on research, the implication was that they had less time and energy for supporting individual students. Contrast this with the position taken by some Midlands university lecturers interviewed as part of a widening participation project who believed that quality assurance measures got in the way of inclusive practice:

> Teachers said that their attempts to adapt their teaching in response to the interests and needs of their diverse student groups had been delayed or frustrated by institutional procedures designed to assure 'quality', or by systems set up to maximise the economic efficiency of teaching.
>
> (David, 2008: 21)

Local factors appeared to be a major element in determining the effect of national policies. Respondents described the particularities of their university culture, the specific events which had shaped their recent history and the climate of individual departments. The idiosyncrasies of particular institutions seem to make a major difference to how national policies are played out and, consequently, the experience that disabled students have of teaching, learning and assessment in each university. An example is the marked institutional difference in awareness of the Postgraduate Diploma in Teaching in Higher Education, which addresses inclusive educational practices. The contrast was most obvious between University 1 (pre-1992), where most staff had not heard of it and believed it was not an institutional priority and University 3 (post-1992) where it was prioritised by senior management.

According to students (and corroborated through staff interviews), even in the same subject, there were major differences in lecturers' willingness to make adjustments and the inclusiveness of their teaching style. There were examples of individual lecturers changing their practices but very few where such changes became embedded in wider practice. The inconsistencies in provision which staff encountered at University 4 (see chapter 9) prompted them to think about how reasonable adjustments were organised and how this could be more effective or fairer. Nevertheless most lecturers were supportive of disabled students and the broad principle of making adjustments to teaching, learning and assessment even though they were sometimes uncertain about what counted as a 'reasonable adjustment', and the extent to which allowances should be made in marking assignments, for example, whether students with a diagnosis of dyslexia should be penalised for errors in spelling, grammar and structure. Not all lecturers subscribed to the implications of anti-discrimination legislation, and particularly in vocational fields of study continued to raise doubts about whether disabled people could ever be 'fit to practise' in areas such as Education.

What is the impact of national policy on institutional policy and practice?

Nationally, marked differences remain between the academic culture and prestige of pre-1992 and post-1992 universities, a mirror of discussions about 'parity and prestige' in a diverse secondary school system (see McCulloch, 2008). Bennett *et al.* (1999) noted that attempts to introduce the teaching of core skills into pre-1992 universities were met with considerable resistance, since these were seen as alien to the traditional knowledge-based culture (see also Dunne *et al.*, 1997). There are also major differences between pre- and post-1992 universities with regard to provision of learning support: Hurst (1996) noting that new universities and further education colleges were far more used to teaching non-traditional students than pre-1992 universities which had to establish learning support services to meet the needs of their newly expanded student population. In our study all four universities were expanding their support for disabled students, but particularly in the pre-1992 universities there were tensions between the demands of research and the need to develop new approaches to teaching, learning and assessment, as noted earlier.

The extensive use of equality audit appears to have had some success in making disabled students more visible to their university. The QAA (2008), for example, notes that 95 per cent of the 129 institutional audit reports published between 2003 and 2006 mention their support for disabled students even though this is not a requirement in the audit. However, 85 per cent of the reports mention disabled students exclusively in terms of 'support', with an institutional focus on encouraging disabled students to 'disclose disabilities before or on entry so that appropriate arrangements can be made to help them reach their full potential' (QAA, 2008: 1). This speaks of higher education institutions which appear not to have moved from a reactive, individualised mode of provision and not to have grasped the significance of the necessity to make anticipatory reasonable adjustments. The new legislation should lead to creating a more inclusive learning environment in which disabled students are not forced to declare an impairment before their needs are met.

From an analysis of the situation in the universities in our study we infer that attempts to alter university policies seem to have been successful as most comply with the legislation in relation to policies concerning teaching, learning and assessment. However, altering policies has not yet resulted in much visible change in practice in teaching and assessment, as can be seen from the staff attitudes, uncertainty about adjustments and confusion about student entitlement which earlier chapters have documented.

Thinking about inclusive educational practice, i.e. offering a range of approaches to teaching, learning and assessment to meet a wide range of learner styles, occurred at an early stage in all institutions. There were major differences within departments in lecturers' willingness to make adjustments, and in the inclusiveness of their teaching style. In some disciplines there was evidence of willingness to make adjustments to pedagogy to accommodate different students' needs, but this was not matched when it came to adjustments in modes of assessment. There is unevenness in understanding disabled students' needs and in the willingness and ability to accommodate to them. It is clear that legislation in itself does not create a higher education environment that accommodates the educational needs of disabled students.

Most adjustments that we noted were formulaic, for example, providing lecture notes in advance and a standard period of extra time in examinations. The problem with such reasonable adjustments is that they are put in place for students with particular impairments rather than being tailored to each one's learning needs. There is a lack of theoretical justification for the type of adjustment amount and no attempt is made to allow for differences in the severity or form of the impairment. The adjustments are blunt instruments rather than carefully calibrated ones to meet an individual student's needs.

Little progress had been made in relation to allowing students to demonstrate mastery of learning outcomes through alternative forms of assessment. Some of the most inclusive practices seem to sit within particular disciplines and not necessarily to have come about because of disability awareness but, rather, as a result of a particular disciplinary culture (see chapter 4).

Enhancing disabled students' learning

Considerable progress has been made in developing policy and provision for disabled students in higher education including the classroom experience but there are still considerable challenges to overcome: trying to change deep-seated and enduring cultures at many levels in universities, a process that is seldom straightforward and often meets resistance (see also chapters 2, 7 and 9). To enable continued monitoring of disabled students' experiences, their retention and academic outcomes, universities need to ensure that they have systems that are fit for purpose. In this study we encountered systems that prevented an analysis of disabled students except in gross terms. We have been unable to comment on important issues like social class, age, type of impairment, ethnicity and subject studied. Without the ability to make these finer distinctions universities are unable to monitor and change their own practices as needed.

According to our survey of disabled and non-disabled students for the most part, disabled students had similar experiences of teaching, learning and assessment as non-disabled students. They fell along a continuum of learner differences and shared challenges and difficulties with other higher education students. However, disability-related barriers had a significant impact on their experiences of learning and assessment in a small number of situations. These barriers emerge in the longitudinal study and still included physical access, despite legislation requiring universities to make their buildings accessible. Other barriers included staff attitudes towards making reasonable adjustments and ways of teaching that made it difficult for students with particular impairments to benefit from the curriculum. Efforts to remove disabling barriers are important and need to focus on developing an inclusive curriculum for all students.

Developing inclusive curricula

Wherever possible the environment for teaching, learning and assessment should be designed so that disabled students do not face barriers and become disabled by that environment. The starting point of an inclusive curriculum is how to make adjustments and choices available for all, not just disabled students. It has already been suggested (see chapter 4) that universal design is one way to pursue this goal. Our survey of disabled and non-disabled students emphasised the variety of student experience and the need for provision which is flexible.

Disabled and non-disabled students had a variety of learning needs which did not easily map onto particular impairments or apply to disabled students only. Students talking about their own learning needs and about strategies which are more or less successful in meeting them contradict the view that there is a clear and straightforward relationship between impairment, barrier to learning and appropriate adjustment. Flexibility in teaching and assessment which is built into universal design could make a significant difference to the volume of individual adjustments that need to be made (though it will not obviate the need for some individual adjustments to meet individual needs). This would appear to meet one of the difficulties expressed by senior managers as well as lecturers that making adjustments is costly and onerous. Greater flexibility in the nature of assessment for *all* students would reduce the need to make adjustments for particular groups and would appear to meet one of the criticisms that students made of special arrangements, that it forced them to adopt a disabled identity and in many cases provided a very visible and unwelcome marker of their difference from other students.

Given the overlap identified here in the learning experiences of students labelled as 'disabled' and 'non-disabled' it is not obvious that disabled students should be treated as a separate category. Disabled students, as non-disabled ones, fall along a continuum of learner styles and learning difficulties so it can be argued as indeed do Shakespeare and Watson and some of the disabled students in this study that we are all impaired in some way:

> We believe that the claim that everyone is impaired, not just 'disabled people', is a far-reaching and important insight into human experience, with major implications for medical and social intervention in the twenty first century.
>
> (Shakespeare and Watson, 2002: 25)

The import of this position is that the impulse to change curriculum and pedagogy in higher education is to create an educational environment that is inclusive for all rather than focusing on a particular group – an issue of fairness that was raised by disabled students and staff alike. In the long run non-disabled students also benefit from the reasonable adjustments put in place as a result of disability legislation. Many of the adjustments introduced to help disabled students, such as well-prepared handouts, instructions given in writing as well as orally, notes put online, and variety and flexibility in forms of assessment, are good teaching and assessment practices which benefit all students. As departments and institutions introduce more flexible learning and alternative forms of assessment for disabled students, demand is likely to rise for giving greater flexibility to all students.

Student support or supportive environments?

Over recent years, UK universities have had to pay serious attention to student support issues, including those associated with transition, as a result of greater diversity within the student population. Certain types of support were becoming mainstreamed across the universities in our study, but in all institutions barriers remained. The findings from this project have a number of implications for how higher education institutions develop their policies and practices to ensure inclusion of all disabled students. It is clear that institutions have, and are continuing to develop, support services for disabled students. It is also evident that students appreciate the support they are offered. However, different types of institutions experience a range of tensions (see chapter 2). For example, we found that teaching in pre-1992 institutions is affected more severely than in post-1992 ones by staff research commitments. Observation of teaching sessions and discussion with lecturers also highlighted cultural differences between academic subjects which varied in the flexibility of their teaching and assessment practices, and in staff beliefs about the ability of disabled students to engage with their teaching subject. The way that support is developed further in these institutions will need to take these tensions and affordances into account.

Much of the support on offer to disabled students is still framed within deficit models. Universities in this project are still caught in the tradition of making adjustments for disabled students as opposed to creating more genuinely supportive learning environments. An inclusive, supportive environment requires an understanding of the pivotal role played for many students of family, friends and fellow students – issues that are highlighted in chapters 7 and 8 especially.

Issues for further action and research

The research discussed here shows that there is a vital need to continue to seek out, listen to and act upon the views of disabled students and of lecturing staff in our attempts to make higher education thoroughly inclusive. By listening to disabled students it became obvious that there were certain issues to do with their time as students which were of great personal importance to them and which were not adequately conceptualised by seeing them solely or predominantly as learners in higher education. Our discussions with staff clarified some of the subject culture differences in perspective and practice, where some aspects of resistance to change reside. We also noted a great deal of thoughtfulness about the issues from them in trying to meet the learning needs of disabled students. In this final section of the chapter we shall look at some of the issues raised by students and staff which we consider worthy of further action and research.

Staff

Staff were particularly concerned about how to obtain the information and the support they required in order to engage in more inclusionary teaching and assessment. Throughout this book runs a common thread, that staff are not sufficiently well-informed about disability legislation or, more importantly, are not confident about how they might perform their duties towards disabled students as a result of that legislation, that university systems lack clarity and what is available for disabled students is not clear to staff.

Better communication between and within central services and academic departments together with more sophisticated understandings about how to create a more genuinely inclusive and supportive environment as opposed to increasing dedicated support services would ensure more effective support for all disabled students, not just those who contact the disability support office. More effective monitoring of the experiences and outcomes of disabled students, by impairment, should lead to the provision of more effective support for those most at risk of academic failure. Disabled students are a heterogeneous group and their experiences and outcomes are variably linked to the nature of their impairment. There should be a greater focus on the development of inclusive curricula, based on the principles of universal design. This would obviate the need for students to disclose an impairment in order to obtain additional support, which was resented by many who did not feel comfortable with being labelled as disabled.

If the concept of universal design as part of developing a truly inclusive learning environment is to take place, it is clear that further research that concentrates on locating barriers and ways to remove them would be vital. In addition, staff development, drawing on the existing good practice that stems from subject cultures is a first priority. Further work is needed to establish how to nurture the supportive environment mentioned earlier that would enable disabled students to flourish without being defined as deficient or especially needy. Disability support officers would need to be involved in this re-definition and re-shaping of support.

Students

For students the main themes that cut across teaching, learning and assessment are to do with identity, transitions, disclosure and the additional 'work' entailed in being a disabled student.

The various ways in which disability as an administrative category impinges on and creates a backcloth for disabled students' conceptualisations of themselves and the nature of their experience as students in higher education is complex and warrants further research as does the issue of transitions.

The relationship between impairment and identity was particularly the focus of chapters 6 and 8 which illustrate that disability as a social category must be seen as another example of a transitional status, varying between contexts and at different points in an individual's biography. The longitudinal case studies showed that some students, particularly those with visible impairments, come to university with disability as part of their pre-established identity. For many, coming to university made them face decisions about how to position themselves in terms of identity. Some adopted disability as part of their identity, albeit reluctantly, during their time at university in order to obtain reasonable adjustments but nevertheless continued to de-emphasise disability in other aspects of their university life. A small number of individuals identified somewhat with the political disability movement, but the majority had severe reservations about the label and did not incorporate disability into their core identity, preferring to see themselves as normal on a continuum of differences that included themselves and 'non-disabled' students. Neither the medical nor the social model of disability was useful in understanding the complexity and contextual nature of students' conceptions of themselves which interwove issues such as difference, normality and diversity.

Students raised issues of 'difference' throughout their interviews: the key point in relation to learning is that fears over being perceived as 'different' by both staff and students could prevent disabled students' disclosure of impairments. Failure to declare could potentially adversely affect their learning as reasonable adjustments would not be put in place in an institution which continued to see its role as involving making accommodations for students with declared disabilities. The knock-on effects of issues in identity and the perceived stigmatising potential of disclosing an impairment meant some disabled students did not ask for and did not receive the learning support and reasonable adjustments to which they were entitled.

Many disabled students, particularly those with mental health difficulties experienced particular difficulties at transitional points in their degree programmes. They had to manage identity shifts connected with disability, as well as more tangible transitions, and they were particularly vulnerable to stress and academic failure at points such as the beginning of a new course or the start of an exam period. For many students impairment had an impact on transitions throughout their university career which is variable and influenced by type of impairment as well as the student's age and social class. Chapters 3 and 7 indicated that most students played down the impact of their impairment and were, in some cases, unwilling to seek the support to which they are entitled. Entry into, transition through and exit from the university posed additional problems for disabled students. They had to make decisions on disclosure at many points, including entry to the labour market, where they had little guidance or support. Disclosure and acceptance of the label of disability was problematic for some students, especially those with unseen impairments.

University systems in relation to disclosure were complex and not transparent as far as disabled students were concerned. They varied from university to university, as already indicated, and between departments. Institutional provision of reasonable adjustments to learning was extremely variable. Students were often not well-informed about when they should disclose an impairment and about the support to which they were entitled, whether in the form of the DSA or other curricular adjustments (see also Fardell and Stead, 2008). Students were unsure about when, to whom and how frequently they should disclose an impairment and were not confident, even when they had disclosed their disability that their learning needs would be met because of inconsistencies in the way information about disabled students was handled. In the survey and in individual interviews, disabled students reported particular difficulties in obtaining the adjustments they had been assessed as needing, and communication between the central Disability Office and individual tutors was often problematic.

There was considerable variation amongst the group of students whom we studied in their ability to engage with the social aspects of university life. This suggests that there is a need to pay greater attention to the social and emotional aspects of learning in higher education, including additional support for vulnerable students at points of transition. The interviews also indicated that students felt best supported in situations where they could build effective personal relationships with academic and support staff and also engage personally and academically with fellow students.

Disabled students experienced the extra burden of emotional work (some already noted earlier) that went with being disabled at university: additional planning and organisation related to the effects of impairment, the provision of support, or actively managing disclosure and the reactions of others. Sometimes disabled students mentioned that this work was hidden and went unappreciated by fellow students and staff. It would be valuable to do further research into the range and extent of this extra work which is a powerful counterpoint to the model of disabled students as in some respects deficient. More importantly, we need to work towards a higher education system that is a more flexible, supportive, transparent and inclusive community which does not impose such burdens on staff or students.

Appendix

Table A.1 Student participants in the four universities, their key characteristics and outcomes as in December 2007

University 1: *Student name*	*Discipline*	*Impairment declared to university*	*Impairment disclosed to project but not to university*	*Self-defined social class*	*Age*	*Outcome*
Jean	Initial Teacher Training	Dyslexia		Working class	30–39	First
Fred	Initial Teacher Training	Dyslexia		Middle class	18–24	Lower second
Lesley	Initial Teacher Training	Multiple: mobility impairment, hearing impairment	Dyscalculia (did not agree to being assessed)	Middle class	25–29	Year out after Year 3 (pregnancy)
Andrew	Initial Teacher Training	Multiple: cerebral palsy, asthma		Working class	18–24	Lower second
James	Geography	Dyslexia		Middle class	18–24	First
Euan	Astrophysics	Mental health		Middle class	18–24	Ordinary degree, unconfirmed
Kathryn	Chemistry	Diabetes		Middle class	18–24	On track – 5-year degree
Teresa	Bioscience	Epilepsy	Mental health	Middle class	18–24	Year out after Year 2 then withdrew from course
Fiona	Zoology	Heart condition		Working class	18–24	Upper second

(continued overleaf)

Table A.1 Continued

University 3: Post-1992

Name	Course	Disability	Social class	Age	Outcome
Darren	IT and Multi-media	Dyslexia	Middle class	18–24	Upper second
Dalia	Multimedia	Mobility impairment, wheelchair user	Middle class	18–24	Not yet graduated – on sabbatical with Students' Union
Duncan	Computing	Dyslexia	Middle class	18–24	Ordinary BSc – upgrade option if submits more work
Dermot	Computing	Epilepsy	Withdrew before asked about social class	18–24	Withdrew from course in Year 2 for employment
Dawn	Geography	Multiple: hearing impairment, dyslexia, dyspraxia, medical conditions	Middle class	18–24	Upper second
Daisy	Heritage and Tourism	Multiple: visual impairment, dyslexia, dyspraxia	Middle class	18–24	Upper second
Divina	Hospitality Management	Dyslexia	Middle class	18–24	Withdrew from course in Year 3
Dionne	Initial Teacher Training	Crohn's Disease	Withdrew before asked about social class	18–24	Withdrew from project during Year 2

(continued overleaf)

Table A.1 Continued

Table A.2 Institution and organisational position of staff referred to in the text of this book

Institution	Staff name	Organisational position
University 1	Adams	Initial Teacher Training (ITT) Lecturer
	Anderson	ITT Lecturer
	Armstrong	ITT Lecturer
	Archer	ITT Lecturer
	Avery	ITT Lecturer
	Aitchison	ITT Lecturer
	Ashcroft	Education Studies (non QTS) Lecturer
	Abercromby	Education Studies (non QTS) Lecturer
	Allen	Sciences Lecturer
	Ashwood	Sciences Lecturer
	Alexander	Sciences Lecturer
	Allison	Sciences Lecturer
	Armitage	Humanities Lecturer
	Allwood	Humanities Lecturer
	Appleby	Modern Languages Lecturer
	Arnold	Senior Manager
	Austen	Senior Manager
	Ackroyd	Senior Manager
	Abbot	Disability Support Officer
University 2	Collins	Senior Manager
	Clark	Senior Manager
	Clements	Senior Manager
	Crossley	Disability Support Officer
University 3	Dennis	ITT Lecturer
	Dawson	ITT Lecturer
	Davidson	ITT Lecturer
	David	ITT Lecturer
	Darton	Computing Lecturer
	Day	Computing Lecturer
	Dover	Computing Lecturer
	Dean	Computing Lecturer
	Dudley	Humanities Lecturer
	Dent	Senior Manager
	Dobson	Senior Manager
	Dalton	Senior Manager
University 4	Black	Technology Lecturer
	Butler	Technology Lecturer
	Bryant	Technology Lecturer
	Brooks	Technology Lecturer
	Brand	Performance Lecturer
	Barton	Computing Lecturer

(*continued overleaf*)

Table A.2 Continued

Institution	Staff name	Organisational position
University 4 *continued*	Bolan	Computing Lecturer
	Bray	Administrator
	Burden	Administrator
	Bennett	Senior Manager
	Bridge	Senior Manager
	Brown	Senior Manager
	Burns	Disability Support Officer

Bibliography

Adams, M. (2007) 'Improving the life chances of disabled people: the role of higher education', Professorial Lecture, Leeds Metropolitan University, 9 May 2007.

Adams, M. and Brown, S. (2000) ' "The times they are a changing": developing disability provision in UK Higher Education', paper presented to Pathways 4 conference, Canberra, Australia, December 2000.

Ainscow, M. (2002) *Making Special Education Inclusive*, London: David Fulton.

Archer, L. (2003) 'Social class and higher education', in L. Archer, M. Hutchings and A. Ross (eds) *Higher Education and Social Class: Issues of inclusion and exclusion*, London: RoutledgeFalmer.

Association of Graduate Careers Advisory Services (AGCAS) (2007) *What Happens Next? A Report on the First Destinations of 2005 Graduates with Disabilities*, Sheffield: AGCAS, Disabilities Task Group. Online. Available HTTP: <http://www.agcas.org.uk/assets/download?file=322&parent=74> (accessed 6 November 2008).

Barnes, C. (1991) *Disabled People in Britain: the case for anti-discrimination legislation*, London: Hurst & Co.

Baron, S., Phillips, R. and Stalker, K. (1996) 'Barriers to training for disabled social work students', *Disability and Society*, 11(3): 361–77.

Baumard, P. (1999) *Tacit Knowledge in Organisations*, London: Sage.

Bennett, N., Dunne, E. and Carre, C. (1999) 'Patterns of core and generic skills in higher education', *Higher Education*, 37(1): 71–93.

Berger, J. and Luckman, P. (1972) *The Social Construction of Reality*, Harmondsworth: Penguin.

Beverton, S. and Riddick, B. (2008) *Strategies for Recruiting People with Disabilities into Initial Teacher Training: research report to the Training Development Agency for Schools*, Durham: Durham University.

Bloomer, M. (2001) 'Young lives, learning and transformation: some theoretical considerations', *Oxford Education Review*, 27(3): 429–49.

Bloomer, M. and Hodkinson, P. (2000) 'Learning careers: continuity and change in young people's dispositions to learning', *British Educational Research Journal*, 26(5): 583–97.

Borland, J. and James, S. (1999) 'The learning experience of students with disabilities in higher education: a case study of a UK university', *Disability and Society*, 14(1): 85–101.

Boud, D. and Falchikov, N. (2007) *Rethinking Assessment in Higher Education: learning for longer term*, London: Routledge.

Boxall, K., Carson, I. and Docherty, D. (2004) 'Room at the academy? People with learning difficulties and higher education', *Disability and Society*, 19(2): 99–112.

Broadfoot, P. (1999) 'Empowerment or performativity? English assessment policy in the late twentieth century', paper presented at the British Educational Research Association Annual Conference, University of Sussex, September 1999.

Broadfoot, P. (2002) 'Editorial. Assessment for Lifelong Learning: challenges and choices', *Assessment in Education: Principles, Policy and Practice*, 9(1): 5–7.

Brown, S. and Knight, P. (1994) *Assessing Learners in HE*, London: Kogan Page Limited.

Burgstahler, S. (2001) 'Universal Design of Instruction (UDI): definition, principles, and examples'. Online. Available HTTP: <http://www.washington.edu/doit/Brochures/Academics/instruction.html> (accessed 13 November 2008).

Christie, H., Munro, M. and Wager, F. (2005) ' "Day students" in higher education: widening access students and successful transitions to university life', *International Studies in Sociology of Education*, 5(1): 3–30.

Christie, H., Tett, L., Cree, V., Hounsell, J. and McCune, V. (2008) ' "A real rollercoaster of confidence and emotions": learning to be a university student', *Studies in Higher Education*, 33(5): 567–81.

Clarke, J. and Newman, J. (1997) *The Managerial State*, London: Sage.

Clarke, J., Gewirtz, S. and McLaughlin, E. (eds) (2000) *New Managerialism, New Welfare?*, London: Open University Press.

Cullen, J., Hadjivassiliou, K., Hamilton, E., Kelleher, J., Sommerlad, E. and Stern, E. (2002) *Review of Current Pedagogic Research and Practice in the Fields of Post Compulsory Education and Lifelong Learning*, London: Tavistock Institute.

David, M. (2008) 'Widening participation in higher education: a commentary by the Teaching and Learning Research Programme', London: TLRP. Online. Available HTTP: <http://www.tlrp.org/pub/documents/HEcomm.pdf> (accessed 17 November 2008).

Deakin, N. (1994) *The Politics of Welfare: continuities and change*, London: Harvester Wheatsheaf.

Deal, M. (2002) 'Disabled people's attitudes toward other impairment groups: a hierarchy of impairments', *Disability and Society*, 18(7): 897–910.

DfEE (1999) 'Circular 4/99', *Physical and Mental Fitness to Teach of Teachers and of Entrants to Initial Teacher Training*, London: DfEE.

DfES (2007) *Fitness to Teach Guidance for Employers and Initial Teacher Training Providers*, London: DfES.

Disability Rights Commission (DRC) (2007) *Maintaining Standards: promoting equality. Professional regulation within nursing, teaching and social work and disabled people's access to these professions*. Online. Available HTTP: <http://www.maintainingstandards.org/files/MS_Report_of_a_formal_investigation_full_report.doc> (accessed 6 November 2008).

Dunne, E., Bennett, N. and Carre, C. (1997) 'Higher education: core skills in a learning society', *Journal of Education Policy* 12(6): 511–25.

Earle, S. and Sharp, K. (2000) 'Disability and assessment in the UK: should we compensate disabled students?', *Teaching in Higher Education* 5(4): 541–45.

East, R. (2008) 'Formative vs summative assessment'. Online. Available HTTP: <http://www.ukcle.ac.uk/resources/assessment/formative.html> (accessed 13 November 2008).

Ecclestone, K. (2007a) 'Lost and found in transition: the implications of "identity", "agency" and "structure" for educational goals and practices', keynote paper presented at Researching Transitions in Lifelong Learning Conference, University of Stirling, June 2007.

Ecclestone, K. (2007b) 'Resisting images of the "diminished self": the implications of emotional wellbeing and emotional engagement in education policy', *Journal of Education Policy*, 22(4): 455–70.

Elton, L. (2000) 'Matching teaching methods to learning processes: dangers of doing the wrong thing righter', presentation to 2nd Annual Conference of the Learning in Law Initiative: learning from experience and the experience of learning, University of Warwick, January 2000. Online. Available HTTP: <http://www.ukcle.ac.uk/interact/lili/2000/elton.html> (accessed 13 November 2008).

Elton, L. (2004) 'A challenge to established assessment practice', *Higher Education Quarterly*, 58(1): 43–62.

Engeström, Y. (1987) *Learning by Expanding: an activity-theoretical approach to developmental research*, Helsinki: Orienta-Konsultit.

Engeström, Y. (1999) 'Innovative learning in work teams: analyzing cycles of knowledge creation in practice', in Y. Engeström, R. Miettinen and R.L. Punamäki (eds) *Perspectives on Activity Theory*, Cambridge: Cambridge University Press.

Engeström, Y. (2004) 'The Activity System'. Online. Available HTTP: <http://www.edu.helsinki.fi/activity/pages/chatanddwr/activitysystem> (accessed 1 August 2008).

Exworthy, M. and Halford, S. (eds) (1999) *Professionals and the New Managerialism in the Public Sector*, Buckingham: Open University Press.

Fardell, J. and Stead, A. (2008) 'Inclusion by degrees: experiences of disabled students on Foundation degrees'. Online. Available HTTP: <http://www.fdf.ac.uk/files/fdf_Inclusion_Report.pdf> (accessed 17 November 2008).

Farwell, R. (2002) 'Higher education provision and the change to a mass system', in A. Hayton and A. Paczuska (eds) *Access, Participation and Higher Education: policy and practice*, London: Kogan Paul.

Fender, B. (1996) 'The role of funding councils', in F. Coffield (ed.) *Higher Education and Lifelong Learning*, Newcastle: University of Newcastle.

Field, J. (2006) *Lifelong Learning and the New Educational Order*, Stoke on Trent: Trentham Books.

Freewood, M. and Spriggs, L. (2003) 'Striving for genuine inclusion – academic assessment and disabled students', in C. Rust (ed.) *Improving student learning theory and practice – 10 years on: proceedings of the 2002 10th Improving Student Learning Symposium*, Oxford: Oxford Brookes University, 353–62.

Fuller, M. and Gravestock, P. (2002) 'Enhancing the learning experience of disabled students', workshop presented at National Disability Team national conference: 'Inclusive approaches to learning, teaching and assessment', Coventry, March 2002.

Fuller, M., Bradley, A. and Healey, M. (2004) 'Incorporating disabled students within an inclusive higher education environment', *Disability and Society*, 19(5): 455–68.

Fuller, M., Hurst, A. and Bradley, A. (2004) 'Disabled and non-disabled students' experiences of teaching, learning and assessment: similarities and differences', paper presented at the 5th International Conference on Higher Education and Disability, Innsbruck, July 2004.

Fuller, M., Healey, M., Bradley, A. and Hall, T. (2004) 'Barriers to learning: a systematic study of the experience of disabled students in one university', *Studies in Higher Education*, 29(3): 303–18.

Gallacher, J., Crossan, B., Field, J. and Merrill, B. (2002) 'Learning careers and the social space: exploring the fragile identities of adult returners in the new further education', *International Journal of Lifelong Education*, 21(6): 493–509.

General Teaching Council for Scotland (GTCS) (2002) *Code of Practice on Teacher Competence*. Online. Available HTTP: <www.gtcs.org.uk/nmsruntime/saveasdialog.aspx?lID=467&sID=1092> (accessed 6 November 2008).

Getzel, E. (2008) 'Addressing the persistence and retention of students with disabilities in higher education: incorporating key strategies and supports on campus', *Exceptionality*, 16(4): 207–19.

Giddens, A. (1991) *Modernity and Self-identity: self and society in the late modern age*, Stanford, CA: Stanford University Press.

Goffman, E. (1990) *Stigma*, Harmondsworth: Penguin.

Goode, J. (2007) 'Managing disability: early experiences of university students with disabilities', *Disability and Society*, 22(1): 35–48.

Gooding, C. (2000) 'Disability Discrimination Act: From statute to practice', *Critical Social Policy*, 20(4): 533–49.

Gorard, S. (2008) 'Who is missing from higher education?', *Cambridge Journal of Education*, 38(2): 421–37.

Gorard, S. and Smith, E. (2006) 'Beyond the "learning society": what have we learnt from widening participation research?', *International Journal of Lifelong Education*, 25(6): 575–94.

Hall, J. and Tinklin, T. (1998) *Students First: the experiences of disabled students in higher education*, Edinburgh: Scottish Council for Research in Education. Online. Available HTTP: <http://www.scre.ac.uk/resreport/rr85/index.html> (accessed 15 October 2007).

Hall, S. (1996) 'Who needs "identity"', in S. Hall and P. du Gay (eds) *Questions of Cultural Identity*, London: Thousand Oaks.

Hall, T. and Healey, M. (2005) 'Disabled students' experiences of fieldwork', *Area*, 37(4): 446–49.

Hall, T., Healey, M. and Harrison, M. (2005) 'Disabled students and fieldwork: from exclusion to inclusion', *Transactions of the Institute of British Geographers*, 27(2): 213–31.

Hayton, A. and Paczuska, A. (eds) (2002) *Access, Participation and Higher Education: policy and practice*, London: Kogan Page.

Healey, M. and Jenkins, A. (2003) 'Discipline-based educational development', in R. Macdonald and H. Eggins (eds) *The Scholarship of Academic Development*, Buckingham, Society for Research in Higher Education and Open University.

Healey, M., Fuller, M., Bradley, A. and Hall, T. (2006) 'Listening to students: the experience of disabled students of learning in one university', in M. Adams and S. Brown (eds) *Towards Inclusive Learning in Higher Education: developing curricula for disabled students*, London: RoutledgeFalmer.

Healey, M., Roberts, H., Fuller, M., Georgeson, J., Hurst, A., Kelly, K., Riddell, S. and Weedon, E. (2008) 'Reasonable adjustments and disabled students' experiences of learning, teaching and assessment', *TLA Interchange 2*. Online. Available HTTP: <www.tla.ed.ac.uk/interchange> (accessed 1 June 2008).

HEFCE (2002) *Mapping resources relating to the learning and teaching of disabled students*. Online. Available HTTP: <http://www5.open.ac.uk/cehep/mapping_project/search.html> (accessed 14 November 2008).

Holland, D., Lachicotte, W., Skinner, D. and Cain, C. (1998) *Identity and Agency in Cultural Worlds*, Harvard, MA: Harvard University Press.

Holloway, S. (2001) 'The experience of higher education from the perspective of disabled students', *Disability and Society*, 16(4): 597–615.

Hounsell, D. and Anderson, C. (2008) 'Ways of thinking and practicing in biology and history: disciplinary aspects of teaching and learning environments', in C. Kreber (ed.) *The University and Its Disciplines: teaching and learning within and beyond disciplinary boundaries*, London: Routledge.

Hurst, A. (1996) 'Equal opportunities and access: developments in policy and provision for disabled students 1990–1995', in S. Wolfendale and J. Corbett (eds) *Opening Doors: learning support in Higher Education*, London: Cassell.

Hurst, A. (1998) 'Disability awareness raising and disability awareness training in higher education in the United Kingdom', in A. Hurst (ed.) *Higher Education and Disabilities: international approaches*, Aldershot: Ashgate.

Hurst, A. (1999) 'The Dearing Report and students with disabilities and learning difficulties', *Disability and Society*, 14(1): 65–83.

Hurst, A. (2006) *Towards Inclusive Learning for Disabled Students in Higher Education – Staff Development: a practical guide*, London: Skill/University of Central Lancashire/HEFCE.

Il'enkov, E. (1982) *The Dialectics of the Abstract and the Concrete in Marx's 'Capital'*, Moscow: Progress.

Irons, A. (2008) *Enhancing Learning Through Formative Assessment and Feedback*, Abingdon: Routledge.

Jacklin, A., Robinson, C., O'Meara, L. and Harris, A. (2007) *Improving the Experiences of Disabled Students in Higher Education*, York: Higher Education Academy. Online. Available HTTP: <http://www.heacademy.ac.uk/assets/York/documents/ourwork/research/jacklin.pdf> (accessed 6 November 2008).

Konur, O. (2002) 'Assessment of disabled students in higher education: current public policy issues', *Assessment and Evaluation in Higher Education*, 27(2): 131–52.

Lam, M. and Pollard, A. (2006) 'A conceptual framework for understanding children as agents in the transition from home to kindergarten', *Early Years*, 26(2): 123–41.

Lang, C. and Robinson, A. (2003) 'The withdrawal of non-traditional students: developing an explanatory model', *Journal of Further and Higher Education*, 27(2): 175–85.

Leathwood, C. (2005) 'Assessment policy and practice in higher education: purpose, standards and equity', *Assessment and Evaluation in Higher Education*, 30(3): 307–24.

Leicester, M. and Lovell, T. (1994) 'Race, gender and disability: a comparative perspective', *Journal of Further and Higher Education*, 18(2): 43–51

Lin, C., Kreel, M., Johnston, C., Thomas, A. and Fong, J. (2006) *Background to the Disability Rights Commission's Formal Investigation into Fitness Standards in Social Work, Nursing and Teaching Professions*, London: Disability Rights Commission.

Low, J. (1996) 'Negotiating identities, negotiating environments: an interpretation of the experiences of students with disabilities', *Disability and Society*, 11(2): 235–48.

McCulloch, G. (2008) 'Parity and prestige in English secondary education revisited', *British Journal of Sociology of Education*, 29(1): 381–89.

Meager, N. and Hurstfield, J. (2005) 'Disabled people and the labour market: has the DDA made a difference?' in A. Roulstone and C. Barnes (eds) *Working Futures: disabled people, policy and social inclusion*, Bristol: Policy Press.

Morley, L. (2003) *Quality and Power in Higher Education*, Maidenhead: SRHE and Open University Press.

National Working Party on Dyslexia in Higher Education (1999) *Dyslexia in Higher Education: policy, provision and practice*, Hull: University of Hull.

Neumann, R., Parry, S. and Becher, T. (2002) 'Teaching and learning in their disciplinary context', *Studies in Higher Education*, 27(4): 405–17.

NCIHE (1997a) *Higher Education in the Learning Society*, London: HMSO.

NCIHE (1997b) *Higher Education in the Learning Society: report of the Scottish committee*, London: HMSO.

Oliver, M. (1990) *The Politics of Disablement*, Basingstoke: Macmillan.

Oliver, M. (1996) *Understanding Disability: from theory to practice*, Basingstoke: Macmillan.

Olney, M. and Brockelman, K. (2003) 'Out of the disability closet: strategic use of perception management by select university students with disabilities', *Disability and Society*, 18(1): 35–50.

Osborne, R. D. (1999) 'Wider access in Scotland?', *Scottish Affairs*, 26: 36–46.

Parker, V. (1999) 'Personal assistance for students with disabilities in H.E.: the experience of the University of East London', *Disability and Society*, 14(4): 483–504.

Paterson, L. (1997) 'Trends in higher education participation in Scotland', *Higher Education Quarterly*, 51(1): 29–48.

Power, M. (1997) *The Audit Society*, Oxford: Oxford University Press.

Quality Assurance Agency for Higher Education (QAA) (1999) *Code of Practice for the Assurance of Academic Quality and Standards in Higher Education. Section 3: Students with disabilities*, London: QAA. Online. Available HTTP: <http://www.qaa.ac.uk/academicinfrastructure/codeOfPractice/section3/COP_disab.pdf> (accessed 6 November 2007).

Quality Assurance Agency for Higher Education (QAA) (2008) *Institutions' Support for Students with Disabilities 2002–06: an outcomes from institutional audit paper for the Advisory Group*, Gloucester: QAA.

Race, P., Brown, S. and Smith, B. (2005) (2nd edn) *500 Tips on Assessment*, London: RoutledgeFalmer.

Reay, D. (2003) 'Shifting class identities? Social class and the transition to higher education', in C. Vincent (ed.) *Social Class, Education and Identity*, London: RoutledgeFalmer.

Reeve, D. (2002) 'Negotiating psycho-emotional dimensions of disability and their influence on identity constructions', *Disability and Society*, 17(5): 493–508.

Richardson, J. (2001) 'The representation and attainment of students with a hearing loss in higher education', *Studies in Higher Education*, 26(2): 183–204.

Riddell, S. (1998) 'Chipping away at the mountain: disabled students' experience of higher education', *International Studies in Sociology of Education*, 8(2): 203–22.

Riddell, S. and Banks, P. (2001) *Disability in Scotland: a baseline study*, Edinburgh: Disability Rights Commission.

Riddell, S. and Weedon, E. (2006) 'What counts as a reasonable adjustment?

Dyslexic students and the concept of fair assessment', *International Studies in Sociology of Education*, 16(1): 57–73.

Riddell, S., Tinklin, T. and Wilson, A. (2002) 'Disability and the wider access agenda: supporting disabled students in different institutional contexts', *Widening Participation and Lifelong Learning*, 4(3): 13–26.

Riddell, S., Tinklin, T. and Wilson, A. (2005) *Disabled Students in Higher Education: perspectives on widening access and changing policy*, London: Routledge.

Riddell, S., Weedon, E., Fuller, M., Healey, M., Hurst, A., Kelly, K. and Piggott, L. (2007) 'Managerialism and equalities: tensions within widening access policies for disabled students in UK universities', *Higher Education*, 54(4): 615–28.

Robson, K. (2004) 'Assessment – The final frontier – Just how valid, reliable and fair are assessments of disabled students?', paper presented to QAA Enhancing the Student Experience in Scottish Higher Education Conference: 'Issues of validity, reliability and fairness', University of Stirling, 7 May 2004. Online. Available HTTP: <http://www.enhancementthemes.ac.uk/events/presentations/20040507.asp> (accessed 17 November 2008).

Scanlon, E. and Issroff, K. (2005) 'Activity theory and higher education: evaluating learning technologies', *Journal of Computer Assisted Learning*, 21(6): 430–9.

Schutz, A. (1932 [1972]) *Phenomenology of the Social World*, London: Heinemann.

Scottish Executive (2003) *Life Through Learning Through Life*, Edinburgh: Scottish Executive.

Scottish Executive (2004) *Medical Standards Consultation*. Online. Available HTTP: <http://www.scotland.gov.uk/consultations/education/medicallyfit.pdf> (accessed 6 November 2008).

Shakespeare, T. and Watson, N. (2002) 'The social model of disability: an outdated ideology?', *Research in Social Science and Disability*, 2(1): 9–28.

Sharp, K. and Earle, S. (2000) 'Assessment, disability and the problem of compensation', *Assessment and Evaluation in Higher Education*, 25(2): 191–9.

SHEFC (2000) *Teachability: creating an accessible curriculum for students with disabilities*, Edinburgh: Scottish Higher Education Funding Council.

Simpson, M. (2005) *Assessment: policy and practice in education*, Edinburgh: Dunedin Academic Press.

Stanley, N., Mallon, S., Bell, J., Hilton, S. and Manthorpe, J. (2007) *Summary of Report: responses and prevention in student suicide: the RaPSS study*. Online. Available HTTP: <http://www.rapss.org.uk/> (accessed 27 May 2007).

Stanley, N., Ridley, J., Manthorpe, J., Harris, J. and Hurst, A. (2007) *Disclosing Disability: disabled students and practitioners in social work, nursing and teaching*, London: Disability Rights Commission.

Stone, D. (1984) *The Disabled State*, Basingstoke: Macmillan.

Stuart, M. (2002) *Collaborating for Change?*, Leicester: NIACE.

Swain, J. and French, S. (2000) 'Towards an affirmation model of disability', *Disability and Society*, 15(4): 569–82.

Thomas, C. (1998) *Female Forms: experiencing and understanding disability*, Buckingham: Open University Press.

Tinklin, T. and Hall, J. (1999) 'Getting round obstacles: disabled students' experiences in higher education in Scotland', *Studies in Higher Education*, 24(2): 183–94.

Training and Development Agency for Schools (TDA) (2007) *Able to Teach*, London: TDA.

Tregaskis, C. (2002) 'Social model theory: the story so far', *Disability and Society*, 17(4): 457–70.

Trowler, P. and Cooper, A. (2002) 'Teaching and learning regimes: implicit theories and recurrent practices in the enhancement of teaching and learning through educational development programmes', *Higher Education Research and Development*, 21(3): 221–40.

Waterfield, J., West, R. and Parker, M. (2006) 'Supporting inclusive practice: developing an assessment toolkit', in M. Adams and S. Brown (eds) *Towards Inclusive Learning in Higher Education: developing curricula for disabled students*, London: Routledge.

Watson, N. (2002) 'Well, I know this is going to sound very strange to you, but I don't see myself as a disabled person: identity and disability', *Disability and Society*, 17(5): 509–27.

Weedon, E. and Riddell, S. (2007a) '"To those who have shall be given?" Differing expectations of support among dyslexic students', in M. Osborne, N. Houston and N. Toman (eds) *The Pedagogy of Lifelong Learning*, London: Routledge.

Weedon, E. and Riddell, S. (2007b) 'Transitions into and out of higher education: the experiences of "disabled" students', paper presented at the Researching Transitions in Lifelong Learning Conference, University of Stirling, June 2007.

Weedon, E. and Riddell, S. (2008) 'Disabled students and transitions in higher education', in K. Ecclestone (ed.) *Lost in Transition: change and becoming through education and the lifecourse*, London: Routledge.

Index